Generously Donated to
The Frederick Douglass Institute
By Professor Jesse Moore
Fall 2000

W9-CJO-258

Student's Review Manual

FOR

John A. Garraty

The

American

Nation

A History of the United States Since 1865

FOURTH EDITION

Ellen Howell Myers

San Antonio College

HARPER & ROW, PUBLISHERS

New York   Hagerstown   Philadelphia   San Francisco   London

Student's Review Manual for John A. Garraty THE AMERICAN NATION
   A History of the United States Since 1865, Fourth Edition

Copyright © 1979 by Ellen Howell Myers

All rights reserved. Printed in the United States of America. No part of this book may be used or reproduced in any manner whatsoever without written permission except in the case of brief quotations embodied in critical articles and reviews. For information address Harper & Row, Publishers, Inc., 10 East 53rd Street, New York, N.Y. 10022.

ISBN 0-06-044711-7

Contents

Introduction   iv

16:   Reconstruction and the South   131

Portfolio Four: The Plains Indians   141

17:   An Age of Exploitation   144
18:   An Industrial Giant   154
19:   The Response to Industrialism   163
20:   Intellectual and Cultural Trends   171
21:   National Politics: 1877–1896   179
22:   From Isolation to Empire   189
23:   The Progressive Era   201

Portfolio Five: Women's Lot   212

24:   Woodrow Wilson and the Great War   215
25:   The Twenties: The Aftermath of the Great War   225
26:   The Great Depression: 1929–1939   234
27:   Isolationism and War: 1921–1945   244
28:   Foreign Affairs: 1942–1964   256

Portfolio Six: The Painter's Eye   267

29:   The Postwar Scene: 1945–1964   270
30:   Modern American Society   281
31:   Vietnam and Its Aftermath   291

Introduction

The purpose of this Student's Review Manual is to help you study and review the textbook *The American Nation* (Fourth Edition) by John A. Garraty. The Manual is not a replacement for or a condensed version of the text, but instead a guide to its major points. The textbook is like a tree: The trunk contains important themes and generalizations, holding together and giving life to the branches of ideas, events, and personalities which have made history. The Student's Review Manual points out the major branches. These facts are useless unless they are attached to a major theme in a meaningful way.

Each chapter of the Review Manual is organized in the same manner. First there is a *Chronology,* which gives a few significant dates of events mentioned in the text. Then comes a *Chapter Checklist,* which summarizes the major points covered. This checklist is followed by a list of *Other Terms to Identify,* which provides further information to help you understand the material. The items are listed in the order in which they appear in the chapter. After *Other Terms* is a *Glossary* with definitions of words and terms that may not be familiar to you, listed alphabetically. Then there is a list of other words you should be able to define and a selection of *Sample Questions:* multiple choice, true-false, and some matching.

To use this Manual for best results:

First, read the assigned chapter in the textbook, keeping the Manual close at hand in order to look up unfamiliar terms or phrases in the *Glossary*. It is a good idea, too, to keep a dictionary nearby in case you need to be sure of the meaning of certain words, particularly those listed under *Words to Know*.

Then, to review the chapter, read the *Chapter Checklist*. You will find, along with the major points, other features such as small charts and *Presidents' Boxes,* the latter outlining important dates and events in the life of each president. *Other Terms to Identify* will help remind you of additional facts covered in the text.

After studying the textbook and the Student's Review Manual, spot-check your memory of the material by answering the *Sample Questions*. They will also give you practice in answering objective questions on quizzes and exams. If you find you cannot answer one or more of the questions, go back to the text and to the Manual for further study.

16

Reconstruction and the South

CHRONOLOGY

1863 Lincoln's ten percent plan
1865 Thirteenth Amendment
1866 Civil Rights Act
1868 Fourteenth Amendment
1868 Impeachment of President Johnson
1870 Fifteenth Amendment

CHAPTER CHECKLIST

Reconstruction. The post-Civil War period, from approximately 1865 to 1877, during which the United States confronted the problems of readmitting the southern states to the Union and integrating the freed slaves into society.

Readmission of the States.

Controversies. Should the southern states be readmitted automatically or should conditions be placed on their admission? If conditions were set, who should determine them, the president or Congress?

1863, Lincoln's ten percent plan. A program for reconstruction designed by Lincoln and based on his presidential pardoning power. All southerners, with the exception of high Confederate officials and a few other groups, could reinstate themselves as United States citizens by taking a loyalty oath. When a number equal to ten per cent of those voting in the 1860 election in a particular state had taken the oath, then that state could set up a state government. The only requirements placed on the new governments were that they be republican, that is, representative; that they must recognize the free status of all blacks; and that they provide for the education of blacks. State governments in Tennessee, Louisiana, and Arkansas were set up under the ten per cent plan, which was very much disliked by the Radical Republicans in Congress.

1864, Wade-Davis bill. Passed by both houses of Congress, this bill would have made readmission difficult. It was disposed of by Lincoln with a pocket veto. It required that a majority rather than ten percent of the voters take a loyalty oath to the Union. Those who had been officials in the Confederate government or had voluntarily fought against the United States were barred from voting in the election or serving in the subsequent state constitutional convention. The requirements for the new constitutions were that they prohibit slavery and repudiate all Confederate debts. This unsuccessful bill was favored by the Radical Republicans.

1865, Thirteenth Amendment. Constitutional change which abolished slavery within the United States. An amendment requires a two-thirds vote in both houses of Congress and ratification by three-quarters of the states.

1867, Reconstruction Act. The southern states, excluding Tennessee, were divided into five military districts, each controlled by a major general with almost dictatorial power. In order to end military rule and be readmitted to the Union, the states were to call conventions and draw up new constitutions which would give blacks the vote and prevent former Confederate leaders from voting. If Congress approved the new constitution, and the state legislature ratified the Fourteenth Amendment, then the state would be readmitted. The southerners got around this act by not calling constitutional conventions. So Congress passed another Reconstruction Act requiring the military authorities who were occupying the states to register voters and supervise the election of delegates to con-

---

ANDREW JOHNSON (1808–1875), 17th President

Born in North Carolina and moved to Tennessee where he entered politics as a Jacksonian Democrat.

Member of the state legislature and of the House of Representatives.

Governor of Tennessee (1853–1857).

United States Senator (1857–1862).

As a southerner loyal to the Union, he was appointed governor of federally occupied Tennessee in 1862.

Vice-president under Lincoln (March 4–April 15, 1865).

President (1865–1869).

Impeached by the House and came within one vote of conviction by the Senate in 1868.

Elected to the Senate in 1874 and died the next year.

stitutional conventions. Southerners defeated the new constitutions by not going to the polls, because the law stated that a majority of registered voters had to ratify the document.

1868, Reconstruction Act. A law stating that constitutions were to be ratified by a majority of the voters, not a majority of those who had registered to vote. Finally Congress got its way, and the rest of the southern states were admitted by 1870.

Radical Republicans and Their Program

Charles Sumner (1811–1874). Leader of the ultra-Radical Republicans who insisted on immediate racial equality. He, along with Thaddeus Stevens, believed that the southerners had committed "state suicide" and should be treated during Reconstruction as conquered provinces. Sumner was senator from Massachusetts from 1851 to 1874, although he was absent for three years while recovering from the caning by Representative Preston Brooks in 1856.

Thaddeus Stevens (1792–1868). A Radical Republican who supported Reconstruction policies which would protect the freedmen and punish the Confederates, although he was willing to compromise to get the votes of less radical Republicans. Stevens represented Pennsylvania in the House as a Whig from 1848 to 1852 and as a Republican from 1859 to 1868.

Benjamin Wade (1800–1878). Senator from Ohio who was a leader of the Radical Republicans. During the Civil War he was chairman of the Joint Committee on the Conduct of the War.

1865–1866, Black Codes. Laws passed in southern states to regulate the legal and employment status of the freed slaves. The codes varied from state to state, and although some represented a considerable improvement over slavery, others were designed to get around the Thirteenth Amendment and placed limitations on their freedom. Some codes recognized marriages and permitted blacks to sue and testify in court and to own certain types of property. But some states also passed codes stating that freed persons could not carry weapons, take jobs other than farming and domestic work, or leave their jobs without losing back pay.

1865–1872, Freedmen's Bureau. A branch of the War Department designed to coordinate efforts to help the freed slaves. Its most important function was helping them in the job market, defending their right to select their own employer, and to receive a just wage. Also the bureau founded schools and provided food and medical care.

1866, Civil Rights Act. A law which declared that blacks were citizens of the United States; the measure overturned the Dred Scott decision (1857) and was later confirmed by the Fourteenth Amendment (1868). The act also tried to negate some of the Black Codes by declaring that states could not restrict blacks' rights to testify in court and to hold property. President Johnson vetoed the bill, feeling that it violated states' rights, but Congress overrode his veto with a two-thirds majority in each House. The

1866 Civil Rights Act was the first major piece of legislation to become law over the veto of a president. Radical Republicans were afraid that it would be declared unconstitutional; so they initiated the Fourteenth Amendment.

1868, Fourteenth Amendment. An amendment passed by Congress in 1866 and ratified by three-fourths of the states in 1868 after the southern states had been instructed in the Reconstruction Act that they would not be readmitted to the Union until they did so. The amendment provided that: (1) all persons born or naturalized in the United States were citizens; (2) no state could "deprive any person of life, liberty, and property, without due process of law;" (3) southern states must grant blacks the vote or have their representation in Congress reduced; (4) former state or national officials who had joined the Confederacy could not hold another office unless specifically pardoned by a two-thirds vote of Congress; and (5) the Confederate war debt was not to be paid. The Fourteenth Amendment was an important milestone in centralizing political power at the national level, for it reduced the power of all the states.

1867, Tenure of Office Act. This prohibited the president from removing officials who had been appointed with the consent of the Senate without first getting the Senate's approval to dismiss them. President Johnson felt this act was unconstitutional and deliberately violated it by dismissing Secretary of War Edwin Stanton, who was in open sympathy with the Radical Republicans. This action gave the Radicals the excuse they had been looking for to impeach Johnson.

1868, Impeachment of Johnson. The president can only be removed from office after being impeached and convicted of "Treason, Bribery, or other high Crimes and Misdemeanors." Impeachment is accomplished by a majority vote in the House of Representatives, and conviction requires a two-thirds vote in the Senate, where the case is tried, presided over by the Chief Justice. Johnson was impeached, that is, charged, on eleven counts, most of them dealing with violation of the Tenure of Office Act. This largely political effort on the part of the Radical Republicans to get rid of Johnson was unsuccessful—barely. The Radicals failed by one vote to rally the two-thirds necessary for conviction.

1870, Fifteenth Amendment. A constitutional change which guaranteed the vote to freed male slaves. It stated that the vote could not be denied "on account of race, color, or previous condition of servitude."

Politics and the Economy in the South

POLITICS

Black Republican governments. Governments in the southern states during Reconstruction in which blacks for the first time participated, generally voting Republican. Although blacks were elected to a number of political positions, the real rulers of the "black Republican governments" were white carpetbaggers and scalawags.

Carpetbaggers. Northerners who came South during Reconstruction and often took advantage of the black vote. They were a varied group: idealists eager to help the freedmen, employees of the federal government, and enterprising adventurers. Carpetbaggers got their name from the fact that they often arrived with their possessions in a carpetbag, an old-fashioned suitcase made out of material which looked like a carpet or rug.

Scalawags. White Republican southerners who during Reconstruction cooperated with the black out of a desire either to help him or to exploit his vote. Some were planters and merchants who had been Whigs, but most were people from areas that had had small slave populations and who had continued to support the Union during the war.

Union League of America. A club used by white southern Republicans to control the black vote. The organization employed secret rituals and symbols to appeal to the black and get him to join. Then he had to swear to support the League list of candidates on election day.

Ku Klux Klan. An organization of white southerners which attempted to counteract the activities of the Union League and drive the black out of politics. The name is based on the Greek word "kuklos," which means "circle." The Klan was strongest from 1868 to 1872 and was a major force in destroying the Radical Republican governments in the South. The Ku Klux Klan, which is in existence today, is descended from a group which organized in 1915. The revived Klan is not only antiblack but also anti-Roman Catholic and anti-Jew.

1870–1871, Force Acts. Laws passed by Congress to protect black voters from the Klan. The acts placed elections under federal rather than local jurisdiction and imposed fines and prison sentences on persons convicted of interfering with a citizen's voting.

ECONOMY

Sharecropping. A system of cultivating the large plantations at a time when there was little cash to pay wages and the freedmen had no money to invest in land or tools. The plantation owner divided up his land into small units, placing a black tenant on each one. In exchange for housing, tools, and other supplies, the black family provided labor. As rent, the sharecropper agreed to turn over a portion, or share, of his crop, usually 50 percent.

Crop-lien system. A method of financing agriculture when money was in short supply. Local merchants extended credit to planters for supplies in return for a lien, or mortgage, on the growing crop. At harvest time the farmer turned over his crop to the merchant who marketed it and returned what was left over after paying off the debt. Generally, the local

storekeeper or banker would insist that a cash crop, such as cotton, tobacco, or sugar, be planted, thus contributing to a one-crop dependency
rather than diversified farming.

ULYSSES SIMPSON GRANT (1822–1885), 18th President

Born in Ohio and graduated from West Point.
Served in the Mexican War.
Resigned from the army and shifted from job to job between 1854 and
    1861.
Became the outstanding Union general in the Civil War and brought the
    war to conclusion at Appomattox.
President (1869–1877).
Believed that Congress should take the lead in running the government,
    which contributed to a weak presidency.
Was personally honest, but his administration was racked with scan-
    dals.

Elections

Election of 1872
Republican: Ulysses Grant
Liberal Republican: Horace Greeley
Democratic: Horace Greeley
Grant, the incumbent, received the Republican nomination. But a fac-
tion of the party, distressed by rumors of corruption and disappointed by
Grant's failure to achieve civil service reform, set up their own party, the
Liberal Republican. Their candidate was Horace Greeley, eccentric
editor of the New York *Tribune*. The Democrats also nominated Greeley,
but Grant carried the election.

Election of 1876
Republican: Rutherford Hayes
Democratic: Samuel Tilden
In this election the electoral votes of three states—Florida, South
Carolina, and Louisiana—were in dispute, with both the Republicans and
the Democrats claiming a majority in each of those states. Recall that the
winner in each state receives all of that state's electoral votes. To decide
who had won, a special Electoral Commission was established, not to be
confused with the electoral college, which was to decide whether the
Republican electoral votes or the Democratic electoral votes would be
accepted from those states. The Commission was made up of five representatives, five senators, and five justices, with eight of them being Republicans and seven Democrats. A vote of eight to seven decided that the

Republicans had carried those states, and Hayes was elected president with an electoral vote of 185 to 184 for Tilden. The election is significant because it was settled by compromises rather than a return to the battlefield.

Compromise of 1877. An informal agreement reached between Democrats and Republicans in which the Democrats consented not to contest the election if they were granted certain concessions. Hayes agreed to withdraw the last federal troops from the South, to appoint a southern ex-Whig to the Cabinet, and to push federal funding of internal improvement projects in the South. Thus a Republican became president, but with the troops gone, the South regained control of its political affairs, became solidly Democratic, and the black increasingly lost the rights he had gained.

OTHER TERMS TO IDENTIFY

John Wilkes Booth (1838–1865). An actor who shot President Lincoln in Ford's Theatre in Washington, D.C., on April 14, 1865. He and his co-conspirators felt they were avenging the South, not realizing that their hopes for a moderate peace lay in Lincoln. Booth was shot and killed two weeks later when forces surrounded and burned the barn where he was hiding at Bowling Green, Virginia.

Andersonville. The largest Confederate prisoner of war camp for Union soldiers, constructed in Georgia in 1864. In the summer of 1864 it contained 32,000 prisoners, and overcrowding and lack of medical facilities led to the spread of diseases from which almost one-half died. After the war the prison's Confederate commander, Captain Henry Wirz, was charged with murder, convicted, and hanged.

"Forty acres and a mule." A slogan widely popular among southern blacks in 1865. The idea was supported by Congressman Thaddeus Stevens who wanted to confiscate the property of leading Confederates and distribute it among the blacks. In reality, little land went into the hands of freedmen, who did not have the money to buy tools nor seeds to plant.

Whiskey Ring. A scandal during the Grant administration involving Grant's private secretary, Orville E. Babcock, who was in collusion with Treasury officials to help a group of St. Louis distillers avoid paying taxes on distilled whiskey. The fraud was eventually revealed, and 283 persons were indicted although most, including Babcock, escaped conviction.

Wormley Conference. A meeting between Republican and Democratic leaders on February 26, 1877, at the Wormley Hotel which led to Rutherford Hayes receiving the disputed electoral votes in exchange for certain concessions to the South.

GLOSSARY

antebellum. The term literally means "before the war." In the United States, it generally is used in reference to the pre-Civil War period.

façade. The face or front of a building or the portrayal of a fake or artificial front or image. When the Electoral Commission met to determine who should receive the votes in the 1876 election, the atmosphere of judicial inquiry and deliberation was a façade. The decision was really made along party lines.

franchise. A privilege or right granted to a person or group by the government, particularly the right to vote. Black males were given the franchise by the 15th Amendment. In recent years the term often refers to authorization by a manufacturer to a dealer to sell his products.

levee. An embankment raised to prevent a river from overflowing. During Reconstruction in the South, tax rates zoomed, but some of the proceeds were used to rebuild crumbling levees. The same word can also be used to refer to a very formal reception, such as President George Washington's inaugural levee in 1789.

maverick. An unbranded or orphaned calf or colt on the range. The term originated with Samuel Maverick (1803–1870), a Texas cattleman who did not brand his cows. The word also refers to someone, particularly in politics, who does not follow the group. Andrew Jackson was considered a maverick.

Thomas Nast (1840–1902). A political cartoonist who was best known for his cartoons on the Civil War era and also on the corrupt Tweed Ring of New York City. It was Nast who created the donkey and the elephant as the political symbols of the Democratic and the Republican parties.

point of order. In parliamentary procedure it is a question as to whether that which is being discussed is in order or allowed by the rules. If an individual wishes to raise such a question, he says, "I rise to a point of order." Such parliamentary procedures were not always adequately understood by elected freedmen who used them in the Black Republican governments.

Saint Sebastian. A young Roman martyr of the 3rd century who was tied to a stake and killed with arrows for having embraced Christianity. According to the New York *Times* in 1877, Justice Joseph Bradley was criticized so vehemently by the Democrats for having sided with Hayes rather than Tilden when the Electoral Commission's vote was counted, that he seemed like "a middle-aged Saint Sebastian stuck full of Democratic darts."

Solomon. King of Israel in the 10th century B.C., who was particularly noted for his wisdom. Even a Solomon would have been hard pressed to judge rightly as to whether the Republicans or the Democrats had really won in 1876 in Florida, South Carolina, and Louisiana.

Tweed Ring. The corrupt political machine in New York City from around 1859 to 1871 which was notorious for its payoffs and kickbacks. William Marcy "Boss" Tweed (1823–1878) was the political boss and was finally jailed for his activities.

"unredeemed" southern states. The states which were still occupied by Union forces and thus had not reconstituted their own state governments.

WORDS TO KNOW

Define the following, using the dictionary if necessary.

chicanery	obloquy
defalcations	pathological
diatribes	progeny
excoriating	recalcitrance
irascible	voracious

SAMPLE QUESTIONS

Multiple Choice

1. Typical of the Northern approach to the problems of the black during Reconstruction:
    a. Black Codes.
    b. Proclamation of Amnesty.
    c. Freedmen's Bureau.
    d. Ku Klux Klan.
2. Radical Republicans favored:
    a. the retention of President Johnson.
    b. severe treatment of carpetbaggers.
    c. harsh enforcement of "Black Codes."
    d. black suffrage.
3. The Radical Reconstruction Act of 1867:
    a. abolished the Ku Klux Klan.
    b. provided for military control of the South.
    c. left intact existing Southern governments.
    d. was favored by President Johnson.
4. The Fourteenth Amendment did all except:
    a. give citizenship to the freedman.
    b. cancel Confederate war debts.
    c. free the slaves.
    d. guarantee payment of the Union war debt.
5. The Union League of America:
    a. kept the blacks from voting.
    b. worked to make the blacks loyal to the Republican party.

c. provided food and clothing to the destitute in the South.
d. elected Lincoln and Johnson in 1864.

Fill in the blanks with the correct term:

1. _____ Term used for Northerners who came to the South during Reconstruction either to help the freedmen or to take advantage of them, and who often tried to manipulate the black vote.

2. _____ Term used for white Southerners during Reconstruction, many of whom had remained loyal to the Union during the war, who cooperated with the "Black Republican" governments.

3. _____ The most famous of the secret organizations formed by white Southerners to intimidate the freedmen and to discourage them from participating in politics.

4. _____ By this law the Radical Republicans planned to limit the power of the president by requiring him to seek the consent of the Senate before he removed officials whose original appointments had required Senate confirmation.

5. _____ The Democratic candidate who would have won the election of 1876 if the Electoral Commission had not awarded all the disputed electoral votes to Hayes.

ANSWERS
Multiple Choice: c, d, b, c, b. Fill in the blanks: 1. carpetbaggers, 2. scalawags, 3. Ku Klux Klan, 4. Tenure of Office Act, 5. Samuel Tilden.

Portfolio Four
The Plains Indians

PORTFOLIO CHECKLIST

An important Indian culture flourished from around 1780 to 1880 on the Great Plains, the flat, treeless region that covers what is today the midsection of the United States. During that time, although tribal patterns had already been influenced by the white man's civilization—horses, guns, and metal tools—the Indians still maintained their unique cultural traditions which disappeared after 1900.

The horse. Horses were introduced to America by the Spaniards and first reached the plains in the 1540s as a result of Coronado's expedition. They were not widely used until the 1700s, however, and then quickly proved to be an efficient means of hunting the buffalo.

Encampments. Indian camps were usually small, for food was too scarce to permit an entire tribe to camp in one spot. Exceptions were made for special occasions such as a tribal festival, a special buffalo hunt, or a war council. The tepees in which they lived were made, moved, and cared for by the women, although the men decorated them. This was one of the few activities of men in the camp, other than feasting and attending tribal meetings.

Nomadic life. A few Indian tribes lived in permanent earthen lodges and farmed, but most were constantly on the move, following the roaming buffalo. Hunting grounds of the various tribed were not well defined, and intertribal contact was frequent, especially for trading purposes. In particular, the nomads bartered buffalo pelts and meat for food products raised by the more settled tribes on the edge of the plains.

The buffalo. The hunt itself was the central act around which the plains Indians organized their nomadic life. It was planned by the chiefs and elders in the early spring, and these plans were carefully followed. Once the buffalo was killed and butchered, almost every part of it was put to some use.

Religion. The Indian believed that all things had spirits and that these spirits controlled the world. His survival depended upon maintaining contact with these powers, and he therefore developed rituals and sought visions in an attempt to keep in tune with the supernatural. The buffalo hunt was accompanied by religious ceremonies because the Indian believed that without the help of the spirits, the herds would not come within range and the hunters would lack courage and skill for the kill.

Life and society. Education for Indian children consisted of learning from their elders how to survive. Young people married when the boy had acquired a certain number of horses to give to the bride's family, and the event was marked by a simple ceremony. Recreation included horse racing and gambling as well as games similar to lacrosse and field hockey. Hunting and making war were also, in part, sports.

War. The Indian's purpose for making war was usually to acquire personal glory and status in his tribe. Young men looked forward to the day when they could join a warrior society and perhaps die bravely in battle. Only occasionally did war have an economic motive, as in the defense of hunting grounds.

Art. Artistic talents were channeled into utilitarian tasks. Women made clothes and utensils decorated with porcupine quills, beads, paint, feathers, and buffalo fur. Men decorated the tepees' exteriors with paintings.

Decline. By 1890 the traditional culture of the plains Indian was becoming extinct as a result of the encroachment of the white man. The latter's lust for land, his diseases, whisky, army, and the slaughter of the buffalo had changed the existence of the Indian. He was forced to abandon his nomadic life and settle on reservations of the United States government.

OTHER TERMS TO IDENTIFY

George Catlin (1796–1872). A painter and writer who specialized in the study of Indians and tribal life. He published a number of books with engravings, including *Manners, Customs, and Condition of the North American Indians* (1841).

Francisco Vazquez de Coronado (1510–1549). A Spanish adventurer who explored from California to Kansas in an effort to find gold and treasures in the mythical "Seven Cities of Cibola." As a result of this expedition, the Indians learned of the horse.

Francis Parkman (1823–1893). Historian who wrote about the struggle between the French and the English for the North American continent. To do so he spent years collecting material among the Indians of the Northwest and then wrote such books as *The Oregon Trail* (1849) and *The Conspiracy of Pontiac* (1851).

GLOSSARY

cantle. The upwardly projecting rear part of a saddle.

lacrosse. A game in which two 10-member teams attempt to send a small ball into each other's netted goal. Each player has a stick (crosse) at the end of which is a netted pocket for catching, carrying, and throwing the ball. Lacrosse originated among the North American Indians.

pommel. The knoblike structure which sticks up at the foot and top of a saddle. The saddles of Indian women had both a cantle and a pommel.

rabelaisian. Similar to the coarse, robust humor of the French monk, physician, and satirist, François Rabelais (1494?–1553).

sinew. Tendon. The Indians used buffalo sinew as thread.

travois. A primitive vehicle of the plains Indians consisting of two trailing poles bearing a platform or net for the load. The forward ends of the poles were attached to a dog or a horse. See the illustration on P4 •7.

WORDS TO KNOW

Define the following, using the dictionary if necessary,

apogee	odoriferous
cosmos	sedentary
equestrian	sequestered

17

An Age of Exploitation

CHRONOLOGY

1869 Transcontinental railroad completed
1876 General Custer's last stand
1882 Chinese Exclusion Act
1887 Dawes Act
1896 *Plessy* v. *Ferguson*

CHAPTER CHECKLIST

Materialism

Laissez faire. A French term literally meaning "allow them to do." It refers to the doctrine that government should not interfere with business. After the Civil War, Americans wanted a governmental policy of laissez faire so that they could pursue the rapid acquisition of wealth without rules and regulations. However, they did not favor laissez faire in its strictest sense, for they eagerly accepted government subsidies such as land grants to railroad companies.

"Gilded Age." Used by Mark Twain to portray the post-Civil War era—dazzling on the surface, base metal beneath; in other words, not solid gold but simply gilt on the surface for show. *The Gilded Age* (1873) is also the name of a novel about the period, written by Twain and Charles Dudley Warner.

Social Darwinism. The application of Charles Darwin's biological theories about the survival of the fittest to men and to the economy. Presumably, if laissez faire were practiced, the most efficient men and businesses would survive and rise to the top.

Plains Indians

1851, Policy of concentration. Various Indian tribes agreed to accept limits to their hunting grounds; that is, they agreed to specific boundaries rather than freely roaming the plains. The policy was designed to cut down on intertribal warfare, but more importantly, it let the government negotiate separately with each tribe when it wanted land or concessions, rather than with a group of tribes who claimed a particular hunting area.

1851, Horse Creek Indian council in Wyoming. A gathering of 10,000 representing most of the plains tribes. At this conference *Thomas Fitzpatrick,* an Indian agent for the United States government, persuaded the tribes to accept hunting ground limits, that is, to adopt the policy of concentration.

1867, Small reservation policy. A government decision to limit further the boundaries of the plains Indians by confining them to two small reservations, one in the Black Hills of Dakota Territory, the other in Oklahoma. Rather than continuing as hunters within their own boundaries, as under the concentration policy, they were to be farmers. At two meetings in 1867 and 1868, held at Medicine Lodge Creek and Fort Laramie, Wyoming, the principle chiefs agreed to give up their traditional way of life. But many tribesmen did not accept the decision and fought a series of battles against the United States cavalry. Even the land granted to the Indians under the Small reservation policy was not strictly preserved for them by the government, especially after gold was discovered in the Black Hills in 1874.

1887, Dawes Severalty Act. A congressional act designed to break up the tribal way of life and make the Indian into a typical American farmer. Tribal lands were split into small units, each head of a household receiving 160 acres. A provision prohibited the Indians from selling their land for 25 years, but shrewd speculators got around this protective measure. Citizenship was granted to Indians who took this private property, moved away from the tribe, and "adopted the habits of civilized life."

1934, Wheeler-Howard Act. An act in which the government went back to a policy of encouraging tribal ownership of lands.

Blacks

1877, Hampton's pledge. Governor Wade Hampton of South Carolina promised to respect the rights of the black under the Constitution. Other southerners repeated this principle, but in practice the civil rights of blacks were slowly eroded.

Poll tax. A tax which had to be paid in order to vote. It kept many poor men, white and black, from voting. The poll tax was abolished by the Twenty-fourth Amendment to the Constitution in 1964.

Literacy test. An exam designed not only to determine if one could read, but whether the prospective voter could understand and interpret the state's constitution. Most states with literacy requirements included an "understanding" clause which said an illiterate person could vote if he could understand a passage of the state's constitution read to him by an election official. Whites generally passed this "test;" blacks did not.

1883, Civil Rights cases. A Supreme Court decision declaring unconstitutional the Civil Rights Act of 1875, which had barred segregation in public facilities. It stated that the Fourteenth Amendment guaranteed the civil rights of blacks against invasion by the states, but not by individuals. Therefore, if a privately owned hotel, theater, or restaurant wanted to deny service to a black, it could do so. This situation was not reversed until the 1964 Civil Rights Act.

1896, *Plessy* v. *Ferguson*. The Supreme Court stated that segregation in public accommodations such as railroads and, by implication, public schools, was legal so long as equal facilities were provided for the races. The decision specifically upheld a Louisiana law which required railroads to be segregated. This "separate but equal" standard was overruled, that is, reversed by *Brown* v. *Board of Education of Topeka* (1954).

Booker Taliaferro Washington (1863–1915). An educator, born a slave, who became the leading black spokesman at the turn of the century. He founded Tuskegee Institute in Alabama, a vocational and agricultural school for blacks, and encouraged members of his race to better their position not by fighting segregation but by learning useful skills and demonstrating their abilities. Today blacks differ in their estimates of Washington, some calling him an Uncle Tom after the character in Harriet Beecher Stowe's novel, and others calling him an early advocate of black power. Note the picture of Washington on p. 427.

1895, Atlanta Compromise. An idea of accommodation rather than confrontation presented in a speech by Washington to a mixed black and white audience in Atlanta, Georgia. Washington stated that blacks would settle for second-class citizenship in exchange for educational and economic opportunities which whites should help provide.

Chinese

1868, Burlingame Treaty. An agreement with China designed to stimulate the immigration of Chinese to the United States. Its chief purpose was to provide cheap labor for the construction of the Central Pacific Railroad. A steady flow of Chinese had been coming to the United States since the early 1850s to work in the gold fields, but after the Burlingame Treaty, the number of annual immigrants doubled.

1882, Chinese Exclusion Act. A congressional act which prohibited Chinese immigration for ten years. Later legislation extended the period. This was the first act in which Congress officially closed America's doors to foreigners. The measure was pushed by labor groups in California which resented Chinese competition for jobs.

Mining

Gold and silver. Veins were discovered in the West from the 1850s through the 1870s in California, Colorado, Nevada, Idaho, Montana, and the Dakotas. Western mining was at its height during the era of President Grant (1869–1877).

Virginia City, Nevada. A typical successful mining town which was based on the wealth of the Comstock Lode and later of the Big Bonanza. The town had 25 saloons before it had 4,000 people, and by the 1870s it was filled with huge, ornate houses built by mine operators who had struck it rich.

Henry Comstock. The prospector who gave his name to the Comstock Lode and who sold his claims for a small portion of their true value. He was typical of the individual successful miner in that he sold out to a large company. Mining by the late 1870s had become big business, requiring large capital investments, heavy machinery, railroads, and hundreds of laborers.

Effects of the gold rushes

The metal bolstered the United States economy, as it was used as a medium of exchange.

A literature about the western mining camps developed, with Mark Twain's *Roughing It* (1872) as the most famous example.

Permanent settlers came West, either to work in mining towns or, as disillusioned miners, to work at other trades.

Political organization of the West developed as the area was first organized into territories and then admitted into the Union as states.

Land

1862, Homestead Act. An act which provided 160 acres of free public land to those who would settle on it and cultivate the acreage for five years. Note the chart "Federal Land Grants, 1850–1900" on p. 432. But the Homestead Act did not make the West an area of small independent farmers because:

Most landless Americans were too poor to move West to claim land or to buy equipment with which to farm it.

Many industrial workers did not have the skills or the desire to become farmers.

Wealthy speculators misused the law to gain large tracts by hiring men to file claims and then taking over the deeds.

The climate and soil of the West were not suited to small-scale agriculture.

1873, Timber Culture Act. An act which permitted individuals to claim an additional 160 acres if they would plant a quarter of it in trees within ten years. However, growing seedling trees on the plains was a difficult task, and only 25 percent of those who filed for land were able to obtain full title to it at the end of the ten years.

1878, Timber and Stone Act. An act which allowed anyone to claim a quarter of a section, that is, 160 acres, of forest land for $2.50 an acre if it was "unfit for civilization." This law enabled lumber companies to obtain illegally thousands of acres of tree-covered slopes in the Rockies and the Sierras by hiring individuals to file claims and then turn over their deeds to the big companies.

"Bonanza" farms. Large landholdings, sometimes tens of thousands of acres, owned by giant corporations. These commercial farms, which could afford the new farm machinery and could demand special shipping rates from the railroad, became increasingly important in the late 1800s.

Railroads

Land-grant railroads. Railroads financed by government subsidies in the form of grants of public land. This method avoided the direct outlay of public funds. The companies raised money by selling the land. Note the chart entitled "Federal Land Grants, 1850–1900" on p. 432.

1862, Pacific Railway Act. This measure established a pattern for land grants to railroads and was particularly designed to encourage the completion of the transcontinental railroad. The law gave the builders of the Union Pacific and Central Pacific railroads five square miles of public land on each side of their right of way for each mile of track laid. The land granted was not in one long strip, but alternated, checkerboard fashion, with land the government retained which was not open to homesteaders. See p. 435 for a picture.

Indemnity lands. Public land which was held in reserve for the railroad companies as alternative acreage in case some of their "squares" in the checkerboard had already been settled. In effect, it prohibited homesteading near land-grant railroads. President Cleveland put a stop to this practice in 1887.

Crédit Mobilier. The construction company which built the Union Pacific railroad. A number of the stockholders in the railroad also owned stock in the construction company and consequently allowed the Crédit Mobilier to charge exorbitant prices for construction since the money would be going into their own pockets. When Congress threatened to investigate the Union Pacific in 1868, *Oakes Ames,* who was a stockholder in both companies and also a member of the House of Representatives, sold Crédit Mobilier shares to important congressmen and government officials in order to smooth the way and avoid an investigation. When these "bribes" were finally exposed by the New York *Sun,* Oakes Ames was censured, that is, officially reprimanded by a vote of the House of Representatives, but the damage had been done. Seventy-three million had been spent for about $50 million worth of railroad construction, and the culprits went unpunished.

1869, Promontory Point, Utah. The point where the transcontinental railroad was joined at a special ceremony on May 10, symbolized by the driving of a golden spike with a silver hammer. See the picture on p. 436. The Union Pacific had built westward from Nevada and the Central Railroad eastward from Sacramento, California.

Cattle

Long Drive. The practice of driving large herds of cattle from their pastureland in the Southwest to railroad centers in the Midwest. The typical "Long Drive" was from Texas over the Chisholm Trail to Abilene, Kansas. From there they were shipped to market, principally Chicago. Note the map "Western Cattle Trails and Railroads, 1850–1893" on p. 438.

Open-range ranching. Raising of cattle primarily on public domain, that is, government-owned land. The ranchers' only need was to own a few acres along a water course. This type of ranching declined rapidly in the late 1880s.

1877, Desert Land Act. This measure allowed anyone to obtain 640 acres in the arid states for $1.25 an acre provided he irrigated part of it within three years. The act was exploited and misused. Wealthy ranchers had their cowhands file claims and then sign the claim over to them. It has been estimated that 95 percent of the claims made under this act were fraudulent, for no real effort to irrigate the land was made.

Joseph Glidden (1813–1906). An Illinois farmer who invented barbed wire in 1874. His invention made cheap fencing possible, and ranchers and farmers began to enclose land, putting an end to open-range ranching.

OTHER TERMS TO IDENTIFY

William Graham Sumner (1840–1910). A professor at Yale University in New Haven, Connecticut, who was a strong believer in the doctrines of Social Darwinism. He did not favor government aid to industries, and felt that if left alone, the most efficient individual would "survive" in every field of human endeavor.

1864, Chivington Massacre. An attack by Colorado militia on an unsuspecting Cheyenne community. It was led by Colonel J. M. Chivington, a minister in private life, who told his troops to kill everyone in the village. The incident is representative of the attacks and counterattacks made by whites and Indians, particularly during the period 1862–1867.

1876, Custer's Last Stand. A battle between the forces of Colonel George Custer and the Sioux Indians at Little Bighorn in Montana Territory. Custer foolhardily decided to attack the 2,500 Sioux with his 264 men, and every soldier died.

Leland Stanford (1824–1893). President of the Central Pacific Railroad and later the Southern Pacific. He was governor of California from 1861 to

1863 and senator from 1883 to 1893. He founded and endowed Stanford University in California.

James J. Hill (1838–1916). Railroad builder and financier who constructed the only transcontinental built without government land grants, the Great Northern, running from St. Paul, Minnesota, to the Pacific. The railroad was economically built and carefully planned and was the only transcontinental to survive the depression of the 1890s without going into bankruptcy.

Texas longhorn. Hardy, wiry, bad-tempered cattle which were bred mostly in Texas. They sometimes had a horn spread of six feet. The longhorn was a cross between the descendants of Spanish cattle and of English breeds.

Major John Wesley Powell. A geologist who published a *Report on the Lands of the Arid Region of the United States* in 1879. In it, Powell suggested that western lands be divided into three classes: irrigable lands, timber lands, and "pasturage" lands. The government should change the basic Homestead Act to correspond to varying conditions. Instead of the usual 160 acres, Powell felt that "pasturage" land should be in units of at least 2,560 acres. However, Congress refused to change the basic land laws in any meaningful way.

GLOSSARY

anthropology. The scientific study of the origin of man and his physical, cultural, and social development. When Congress tried to change the Indian by legislation, with measures such as the Dawes Severalty Act, from a nomadic hunter accustomed to communal ownership into a small agricultural capitalist, it was obvious that congressmen of that era knew little about anthropology.

carbine. A light shoulder rifle with a short barrel. It was used by the United States cavalry in Indian skirmishes after the Civil War.

checkmate. A move in the game of chess in which the opponent's king is "attacked" in such a manner that no escape or defense is possible, thus ending the game. In everyday language, the term also means "to defeat completely." General Sheridan once testified that 50 Indians could often "checkmate" 3,000 soldiers.

"Buffalo Bill" Cody (1846–1917). A professional buffalo hunter on the western frontier who later organized a Wild West Show which he toured throughout America and Europe.

Colt revolver. A pistol patented by Samuel Colt (1814–1862) in 1835–1836. Although his original attempt to manufacture it was a financial failure, an order by the government in 1847 for 1,000 revolvers to be used in the Mexican War reversed Colt's fortunes. The pistol became so popular that sometimes the term Colt was used indiscriminately for any type of revolver.

faro. A card game which was popular in gambling houses of the West in the 19th century. Faro is an adaptation of the word "pharoah," because in old French cards the king of hearts was supposed to represent the Egyptian pharoah. In the game, players indicate on the table marked with representatives of the 13 cards of the spade suit which card they believe will win or lose. The dealer then takes two cards from the dealing box; the first loses, the second wins.

fossil. A remnant of an animal or plant of a past geological age, such as a skeleton, footprint, or leaf imprint, embedded in the earth's crust. Othniel Marsh, a Yale professor, dug for fossils on a Sioux reservation.

greenhorn. A recent arrival or inexperienced person. Originally the term referred to a young animal with immature horns. In 1859 the gold rush at Pikes Peak in Colorado attracted the experienced California prospectors along with the "greenhorns" from every corner of the globe.

guerrilla warfare. Acts of harassment by a small band against a military force or government. The term "guerrilla" is the Spanish word for "little war." During the 1860s conflict between the Indians and the militia developed into guerrilla warfare.

Hereford. A breed of beef cattle developed in Herefordshire, a county in England. The cattle have reddish coats with white markings. As open-range ranching began to flourish, pedigreed, that is, purebred, Hereford bulls were introduced into the Texas herds to improve the stock.

hurdy-gurdy. A portable musical instrument, such as a barrel organ, which is played by turning a crank. In Deadwood, where hurdy-gurdies were used in the dance halls, the music was noisier than in many western towns.

Indian Territory. A United States territory which is now part of Oklahoma. It was created as a refuge for Indians by a congressional act of 1834 and ceased to exist in 1907 when Oklahoma became a state.

ledger. A book in which the monetary transactions of a business are recorded. After the Civil War more and more people left their farms and moved to the city, supporting themselves by scratching out accounts in ledgers, that is, working in businesses.

nit. The egg of a parasitic insect, such as that of a louse. Before attacking a Cheyenne community at Sand Creek, Colorado, Colonel J. M. Chivington ordered his troops to kill all ages and made the comparison, "Nits make lice," meaning little Indians grow up.

paleontologist. One who studies fossils and ancient life forms. Professor Othniel Marsh, a Yale paleontologist, was called "Big Bone Chief" by the Sioux Indians.

plain. An extensive, level, treeless land area. In 1860 around a quarter of a million Indians lived on the grass-covered plains between the Rockies and eastern Kansas and Nebraska.

poach. To trespass on another's property, often to take fish or game. Ranchers in the West poached on the public domain in order to have enough grass for their cattle.

quartermaster. A military officer responsible for food, clothing, and military equipment of troops. Not all quartermasters in the West were honest or respectful of the rights of Indians in their area. A quartermaster in the Apache country in New Mexico took 12,000 pounds of corn from the meager supplies set aside for Indian relief.

Walter Prescott Webb (1888–1963). A scholar of the American West who was a professor of history at the University of Texas. His works included *The Great Plains* (1931) and *The Great Frontier* (1952).

wet-nurse. A woman who suckles another woman's child. The term used as a verb also means to treat another with excessive care. The sugar magnate Henry O. Havemeyer told an investigating committee that the buyer, the consumer, should beware. "You cannot wet-nurse people from the time they are born until the time they die," he said.

windfall. Something that has been blown down by the wind, as ripened fruit. The term also means an unexpected stroke of good fortune. By the late 1880s, the "primary windfalls" of the West—the furs, gold and silver, the forests, the cattle, the grasslands—had already been snatched up.

WORDS TO KNOW

Define the following, using the dictionary if necessary.

auriferous	prodigality
debauchery	sagacious
ephemeral	sequestered
harbingers	unctuous
mawkish	venal

SAMPLE QUESTIONS

Multiple Choice

1. "Survival of the fittest" is a term frequently used in describing:
   a. anarchism.
   b. Social Darwinism.
   c. socialism.
   d. laissez faire.
2. The Atlanta Compromise concerned attitudes toward:
   a. Indians.
   b. Chinese.
   c. blacks.
   d. goldminers.
3. *Plessy* v. *Ferguson* (1896) confirmed:
   a. segregation, with its "separate but equal" clause.

b. state regulation of railroads.

c. the reservation policy for Indians.

d. federal control of interstate commerce.

4. The first federal measure to restrict immigration was passed in May 1882:

   a. to stop immigration from Italy and Ireland.

   b. to restrict the number of entry ports in the United States.

   c. to prohibit Mexicans and Canadians from freely crossing the border.

   d. to exclude the Chinese.

5. To help build a transcontinental railway, Congress:

   a. chartered the Crédit Mobilier construction company.

   b. employed Union war veterans and Chinese coolies.

   c. bought most of the stock of the Union Pacific Railroad.

   d. made large grants of public lands to the railroad companies.

True-False

1. Laissez faire is a government policy of noninterference in business.
2. The Dawes Act established the small reservation policy and moved Indians into the Dakota and the Indian Territories.
3. Booker T. Washington urged blacks to devote their energies to learning useful skills rather than fighting segregation.
4. Oakes Ames was the inventor of barbed wire.
5. Open-range ranching consisted of grazing cattle on land which had already been claimed by homesteaders.

ANSWERS

Multiple Choice: b, c, a, d. True-False: T, F, T, F, F.

18

An Industrial Giant

CHRONOLOGY

1867 Grange founded
1877 *Munn* v. *Illinois*
1887 Interstate Commerce Act
1890 Sherman Antitrust Act
1895 *U.S.* v. *E. C. Knight Company*

CHAPTER CHECKLIST

Railroads

Stimulator of the economy

Purchased railroad cars and locomotives, which created thousands of jobs.

Used huge quantities of iron and steel, which fostered that industry.

Encouraged regions to develop their resources, such as the iron industry in Alabama, so as to create traffic for the railroad.

Opened up new areas of settlement by selling their land grants cheaply and on easy terms.

Increased immigration by sending agents to Europe to drum up prospective settlers who might purchase railroad land.

Accelerated technological advances, such as Westinghouse's air brake.

Fostered a telegraph network by allowing Western Union to string wires along the railroad right of way in exchange for free telegraphic service.

Railroad Business Practices

Rebates. Secret, unofficial reductions in railroad rates which were granted to special customers. The railroad owners did not like this practice but felt forced to make concessions in order to obtain large shipping contracts.

Drawbacks. Rebates given to large shippers on the business of the shippers' competitors. For example, Standard Oil not only got rebates on its own freight but also collected 20 cents from the Cleveland railroads for each barrel of "independent" oil they transported.

Long-and-short-haul rate differences. Rates along tracks where no competition existed were often higher than rates on longer distances where there was competition. For example, in the 1870s it cost 30 cents to ship a barrel of flour from Rochester, New York, to New York City, a distance of 350 miles. At the same time, the freight on a barrel of flour going from Minneapolis to New York, a distance of over 1,000 miles, cost only 20 cents because there were competitive railroad lines on that route.

Important Owners

"Commodore" Cornelius Vanderbilt (1794–1877). A self-made man who earned his fortune running steamboat lines, and then in his late sixties turned to railroads. He did not construct new lines, but gained control of rundown railroads which he improved and added to his network. By the 1870s his system stretched from New York to the major cities of the Midwest.

Jay Gould (1836–1892). Financier and railroad owner who was a millionaire before he was 21. He juggled ownership of half a dozen railroads, buying mismanaged companies, combining them with others, and then selling the package deal at a profit. He displayed a grasp of the importance of integration of railroad lines, and by 1890 was reputed to own half the railroad mileage of the Southwest. He also owned several New York lines and controlled Western Union.

J. Pierpont Morgan (1837–1913). An investment banker who became involved in reorganizing major industries such as railroads and steel. In the 1880s he negotiated a "peace settlement" among the major eastern trunk lines, bringing a measure of stability to that competitive jungle while at the same time centralizing financial control in his hands. In 1901 Morgan purchased Carnegie Steel Company and merged it with competing firms to form the U.S. Steel Corporation. Note the photograph of Morgan on p. 454.

Railroad Regulation

1870s, Granger laws. Acts passed in various state legislatures to regulate the rates for railroad and grain elevators. These laws were pushed by a farmers' organization, the National Grange of the Patrons of Husbandry, whose members won control of several state legislatures in the 1870s.

1877, *Munn v. Illinois*. A Supreme Court decision upholding Illinois laws regulating grain elevator and railroad rates. It stated that any business that served a public interest, such as a railroad or grain warehouse, was subject to state control. Having maximum rates set for them did not mean that they were being deprived of property without due process of law.

1886, Wabash case. A Supreme Court decision declaring unconstitutional an Illinois regulation outlawing the long-and-short-haul rate difference. The Illinois law had been applied to the Wabash, St. Louis, and Pacific Railroad and the uneven rates it charged from various Illinois towns to New York. The Supreme Court stated that the Illinois law was attempting to regulate interstate rather than just intrastate trade and that it could not do so.

1887, Interstate Commerce Act. A national law designed to fill the vacuum pointed out by the Wabash case. It stated that all charges made by railroads "shall be reasonable and just," and that rebates, drawbacks, and long-and-short-haul rate differences were unlawful. Railroads were required to publish their rates and were forbidden to change them without due public notice. Most important, the act set up the Interstate Commerce Commission, the first national regulatory commission and the model for later ones. Five members sat on a board to hear complaints and supposedly supervise the affairs of the railroads, although actually they had little power. The Commission could not fix rates, only bring railroads into court when it considered rates unreasonably high. Such cases could be complicated and were often decided in favor of the railroad.

Other Industries

Iron and steel. An industry whose growth was made possible by huge supplies of iron ore in the United States and the coal necessary to fire the furnaces which refined it. Steel, a special form of iron, became commercially feasible with the introduction of the Bessemer process and the open hearth method, both techniques which enabled steel to be mass-produced, beginning in the 1860s. Pittsburgh, Pennsylvania, became the leading steel center. Note the chart "Iron and Steel Production, 1870–1900" on p. 448.

Andrew Carnegie (1835–1919). A Scottish immigrant whose Carnegie Steel Company dominated the industry by 1890. In 1901 he sold out to J. P. Morgan and devoted the rest of his life to philanthropy. Carnegie's "Gospel of Wealth" held that a concentration of wealth was necessary if humanity was to progress, but that rich men should use their money for public benefit. Accordingly, he endowed libraries, public buildings, and foundations, and managed to dispose of 90 percent of his wealth before he died.

Petroleum. An industry which came into existence after Edwin L. Drake drilled the first successful oil well in Pennsylvania in 1859. Originally the most important petroleum product was kerosene, which was used in lamps. Later, the invention of the gasoline engine and the automobile created a need for other products. By the 1870s the fastest growing oil-refining center was Cleveland.

John Davison Rockefeller (1839–1937). An industrialist who created the

Standard Oil empire. Rockefeller knew little about the technology of petroleum, but he was a master at cutthroat competition, and by buying and merging over 70 companies he created the Standard Oil Trust, or monopoly. In later years Rockefeller turned to philanthropy and gave over $550 million to the University of Chicago and four foundations. Note the picture of Rockefeller on p. 457.

Telephone. An industry made possible by Alexander Graham Bell's invention of the telephone in 1876. He thought of his idea in terms of a "speaking telegraph," using electrified metal disks to convert sound waves into electrical impulses and back into sound waves. By 1900, the American Telephone and Telegraph Company, a consolidation of over 100 local systems, dominated the business.

Alexander Graham Bell (1847–1922). A Scottish immigrant whose work with education of the deaf led to the invention of the telephone. He organized Bell Telephone Company in 1877.

Electric light. This industry was the result of Thomas Edison's perfection of the idea of producing light by passing electricity through a thin filament in a vacuum. In 1882 the Edison Illuminating Company opened a power station in New York to supply current for lighting. The Edison system employed direct current at low voltages, but technicians soon found a more effective method. Consequently George Westinghouse founded the Westinghouse Electric Company in 1886, using high-voltage alternating current which has since become standard.

Thomas Edison (1847–1931). An inventor who took out over 1,000 patents in his lifetime for such devices as the incandescent light bulb, the phonograph, the motion-picture projector, and the mimeograph. His research laboratory was at Menlo Park, New Jersey, but he organized many companies to manufacture and sell his products, and most of them ultimately became part of the General Electric Company. The "Wizard of Menlo Park" was famous for the saying, "Genius is two percent inspiration and ninety-eight perspiration." Note the picture of Edison on p. 451.

Radical Reformers

Henry George (1839–1897). A California newspaperman who in 1879 published *Progress and Poverty,* an attack on the distribution of wealth in the United States. George noticed men buying property, waiting for people to move to the area and develop other property near it, and then selling the land at a large profit. What made the land more valuable was people near it, not improvements on it. Consequently Henry George proposed a "Single Tax" which would give the "unearned" wealth back to the people through the government. He felt the Single Tax revenue would be so great that no other taxes would be needed. Single Tax clubs sprang up all over the United States, and in 1886 George ran for mayor of New York City, losing by a narrow margin, but polling better than Theodore Roosevelt, another candidate in this election.

Edward Bellamy (1850–1898). An author who published his most famous novel, *Looking Backward, 2000–1887,* in 1888. The novel described the United States in the year 2000 as a socialist state, that is, with all economic activity carefully planned by the government and all men sharing equally in its wealth. He felt that the 19th century setup benefited only a small number, that industrial ownership would continue to be concentrated in the hands of the few, and that eventually there would be one monstrous trust controlling the economy. Then nationalization would take place, that is, the government would take over all industries; they would be owned by the nation. Supporters of Bellamy's ideas founded over 150 "Nationalist Clubs," but they did not get involved in politics.

Henry Demarest Lloyd (1847–1903). A journalist whose most famous work, *Wealth Against Commonwealth,* published in 1894, was an attack on the practices of the Standard Oil Company. In addition to criticizing Rockefeller's tactics, Lloyd also denounced prevalent ideas of the time, such as Social Darwinism and the laissez-faire philosophy.

Regulation

1890, Sherman Antitrust Act. A congressional act designed to break up monopolies and restore competition. Any combination "in restraint of trade or commerce among the several states, or with foreign nations," was illegal. Persons who formed the combinations or monopolies could be fined $5,000 and sentenced to a year in jail. The law was not effectively used against business monopolies until the administration of President Theodore Roosevelt (1901–1909). At one point, the act was used against labor unions. In the Pullman Strike of 1894, the union was accused of unlawfully restraining trade and thus violating the Sherman Antitrust Act.

1895, *United States* v. *E. C. Knight Company*. A Supreme Court decision which temporarily took the teeth out of the Sherman Antitrust Act. The American Sugar Refining Company purchased the E. C. Knight Company and other sugar refineries until it controlled 98 percent of the sugar refining in the United States. The government took them to court, charging them with violating the Sherman Antitrust Act. The Supreme Court, however, ruled that the company was engaged in manufacturing, whereas the Sherman Act outlawed restraint of trade or commerce. It stated that manufacture and commerce were two different things and only commercial monopoly was illegal. Within a few years, however, the Court reinterpreted the act to include manufacturing.

OTHER TERMS TO IDENTIFY

Henry Bessemer (1813–1898). An English inventor who in the 1850s developed a converter which could make steel from iron in large quantities at an inexpensive price. An American inventor, William Kelly of Kentucky, discovered the technique at about the same time, but it was Bessemer's converter that came into general use.

Mesabi range. A range of low hills in Minnesota known for its deposits of iron ore. The Mesabi iron was discovered by Leonidas Merritt and his brothers in 1887, but in 1893 the area was bought by John D. Rockefeller. The iron was sent from Minnesota to Pittsburgh, Pennsylvania, the steel capital, by way of steamers down the Great Lakes to rail lines from Cleveland and other Lake Erie ports.

George Westinghouse (1846–1914). An inventor and manufacturer who filed over 400 patents in his lifetime. He invented the compressed air brake which made high-speed rail transportation safe by giving complete control of the train to the engineer rather than having separate brakes and brakemen on each car. Also, under his direction, transformers were developed that made possible the high-voltage alternating-current system of distributing electricity. This system proved to be superior to Edison's and is the one in use today. In 1886 he organized the Westinghouse Electric Company.

Trust. A combination of firms or corporations for the purpose of reducing competition and controlling prices throughout a business or industry, that is, a monopoly. The first trust was the Standard Oil Company, and the legal mechanism was worked out by Samuel C. T. Dodd, a Pennsylvania lawyer, in 1882. Standard Oil's original purpose for forming the trust was not to achieve a monopoly (they already had that) but to centralize the management of its diverse operations.

National Grange of the Patrons of Husbandry. An organization founded in 1867 by Oliver Kelley to provide social and cultural benefits for isolated rural communities. The Grange members became inovlved in state politics in the 1870s and won control of a number of state legislatures in the West and South. The "Granger laws" which they passed regulated railroad and grain elevator rates.

GLOSSARY

bung. A stopper for the hole through which a barrel is filled or emptied. An example of Rockefeller's attention to details is the fact that he insisted that the manager of one of his refineries account for 750 missing barrel bungs.

feeder line. A railroad track that connected smaller communities with the main line. Railroad companies spread out feeder lines to draw business to their main lines the way the root network of a tree draws water into its trunk.

forte. Something in which a person excels, a strong point. Rockefeller's forte was meticulous attention to detail.

incandescent. Emitting visible light as a result of being heated. Edison's incandescent lamp produced light by passing electricity through a thin carbonized filament in a vacuum.

ingot. A mass of metal cast into some convenient shape for storage or transportation. Later it is remelted to be shaped into a finished product. By 1880 Carnegie's company turned out about a quarter of the nation's steel ingots.

kingpin. In the game of bowling, the foremost or central pin of the arrangement of pins to be knocked down. The term also refers to the most important or essential person in an activity. The kingpin of the steel industry was Andrew Carnegie.

Mennonite. A member of a Protestant Christian sect which is opposed to taking oaths and to serving in the military. In 1874, 1,900 Mennonites came to Kansas from Russia to settle on land of the Atchison, Topeka, and Santa Fe Railroad.

rolling stock. The wheeled vehicles, the car and locomotives, of a railroad. In 1869 railroads bought $41.6 million worth of cars and locomotives. Railroads continued to expand, and in 1889 they bought rolling stock valued at $90.8 million.

siding. A short section of railroad track connected by switches to a main track. In order to compete, railroads granted favors to certain shippers, such as building sidings at the plants of important companies without charge.

spur line. A short side track that connects with the main track of a railroad system.

transformer. A device used to transfer electric energy, usually that of an alternating current, from one circuit to another.

trunk line. The main line or lines of a transportation system. The transcontinental railroad lines were trunk lines from the start.

utopia. A goal or ideal, often impractical, for social or political reform. The term comes from the imaginary "perfect" island described by Sir Thomas More in his book entitled *Utopia* (1516). Edward Bellamy's *Looking Backward, 2000–1887* was a utopian novel.

WORDS TO KNOW

Define the following, using the dictionary if necessary.

acoustics	emasculated
altruistic	fiduciary
anomaly	naphtha
atypical	nihilist
autocracy	polemic

SAMPLE QUESTIONS

Multiple Choice

1. The Granger laws did *not* attempt to:
   a. bring the railroads under public or state ownership.
   b. set maximum railroad rates.
   c. prevent discriminatory practices by the railroad.
   d. set rates for storing grain.
2. *Munn* v. *Illinois* involved the legality of:
   a. a state attempt to regulate labor unions.
   b. a federal attempt to suppress strikes.
   c. a federal attempt to regulate the Standard Oil Company.
   d. a state attempt to regulate railroads.
3. The Interstate Commerce Act provided for all but which one of the following?
   a. prohibited rebates and pools.
   b. required railroads to publish their rate schedules.
   c. established a commission to hear complaints from shippers and to examine witnesses.
   d. fixed rates that railroads should charge and saw to the enforcement of them.
4. Henry George would have cured society's ills by means of:
   a. anarchism.
   b. socialism.
   c. establishing one large monopoly.
   d. a single tax on land.
5. The primary purpose of the formation of trusts during the latter part of the 19th century was to increase profits by:
   a. lowering interest rates.
   b. making available a greater variety of raw materials.
   c. evading the taxes on private incomes.
   d. eliminating competition.

Matching

1. ____Andrew Carnegie   a. *Looking Backward, 2000–1887*
2. ____John D. Rockefeller   b. telephone
3. ____J. P. Morgan   c. *Progress and Poverty*
4. ____Henry George   d. railroads
5. ____Henry Demarest Lloyd   e. U.S. Steel Corporation

6. ____ Edward Bellamy   f. "Gospel of Wealth"
7. ____ Thomas Edison   g. electric light
8. ____ Cornelius Vanderbilt   h. air brake
9. ____ George Westinghouse   i. oil
10. ____ Alexander Graham Bell   j. *Wealth Against Commonwealth*

19

The Response to Industrialism

CHRONOLOGY

1886 AFL founded
1886 Haymarket Square demonstration
1889 Jane Addams founded Hull House
1892 Homestead strike
1894 Pullman strike

CHAPTER CHECKLIST

Labor Organizations

National Labor Union. A federation of unions created in 1866 whose leaders were basically out of touch with the needs and desires of the workers. A major objective was the formation of worker-owned cooperatives.

Knights of Labor. An organization formed in 1869 by Uriah Stephens which grouped workers into one big union, rather than separating them by crafts. All types of workers were accepted: blacks, women, immigrants, and unskilled laborers as well as craftsmen. The eight-hour day was a major goal, and by 1886, under the leadership of Terence Powderly, the union boasted over 700,000 members. Bad publicity for labor, generated by the Haymarket riot with which it had no connection, caused the union's decline in the late 1880s.

American Federation of Labor. A union of skilled workers organized by craft by Adolph Strasser and Samuel Gompers in 1886. They concentrated on such issues as higher wages and shorter hours, and the strike was their chief weapon. The American Federation of Labor still exists in conjunction with the Congress of Industrial Organizations (AFL-CIO) with which it merged in 1955.

Labor Protests and Strikes

1886, Haymarket Square demonstration. A protest meeting in Chicago called by anarchists after a striker was killed at McCormick Harvesting Machine Company. Police moved in to disperse the crowd, and someone threw a bomb in their midst, killing seven policemen and injuring over 60 others. The anarchists who had organized the demonstration were arrested and condemned to death, even though the person who hurled the bomb was never identified. As a result of this incident, the labor movement, and particularly the Knights of Labor, was branded as radical and lost popular support.

1892, Homestead strike. A five-month walkout at Carnegie's steel plant near Pittsburgh. A major clash occurred when strikers attacked 300 private guards of the Pinkerton agency who had been hired to protect the strikebreakers, that is, men who had been brought in to work while the strike was on. Seven guards were killed, and the company decided to break the 24,000-member Amalgamated Association of Iron and Steel Workers which was supporting the strike. They effectively did so, and labor in the steel industry remained unorganized until the 1930s.

1894, Pullman strike. A strike at George Pullman's Palace Car factory outside Chicago to protest a series of wage cuts. After the strike had dragged on for weeks, the American Railway Union, headed by *Eugene Debs,* voted not to handle trains with Pullman cars. The railroad owners, through their General Managers' Association, appealed to President Cleveland to send in troops to preserve order, and Cleveland did so on the pretext that the mail must go through. The strike was broken by a court injunction.

The Pullman strike had three important results. It demonstrated the power of the courts to break strikes by injunction, that is, a court order demanding that the strikers return to work. If they refused, they were subject to fines and imprisonment. Second, the court order was based on the Sherman Antitrust Act, stating that the union was a combination in restraint of trade. And finally, Eugene Debs refused to obey the injunction and was put in jail. While there he was visited by leading socialists and read their literature, and as a result, became an active socialist in 1897, running for president five times on the Socialist party ticket.

Immigration

1882, Exclusion Act. An act which prohibited Chinese immigration for ten years and also excluded criminals, lunatics, and other persons likely to become public charges. Before this measure, entry into the United States had been almost unrestricted.

1885, Foran Act. An act which outlawed the practice of companies bringing in skilled craftsmen from foreign countries and placing them under contract. The company advanced the money for passage and then collected it in installments from the craftsman's paycheck. This ban on importing contract labor was not every effective.

Padrone system. A method used by the Greeks and Italians to bring in unskilled immigrants. The *padrone* was a contractor who agreed to supply gangs of unskilled laborers to a company for a lump sum. In turn, he would take the sum and pay the workers. By bringing over immigrants who were unfamiliar with the higher wages here, he could pay them low salaries and have plenty left for himself.

"New immigrants." A term referring to immigrants from southern and eastern Europe who came in great numbers between 1880 and 1910. Culturally they were different from the majority of earlier immigrants from northern and western Europe. Note the chart "Immigration, 1865–1915" on p. 475.

American Protective Association. A nativist, or antiforeign, organization founded in 1887 to protest the increasing number of Roman Catholic immigrants. The APA was strongest in the Middle West.

City Slums and Politics

How the Other Half Lives **(1890).** A book written by Jacob Riis, a New York reporter, vividly describing life in the slums. See the photograph by Riis on p. 478.

"Big Tim" Sullivan. Ward boss, that is, neighborhood political leader, of New York's lower east side. In exchange for political support of his candidates, he provided a number of services for the forgotten immigrants in his area, including job placement, Christmas dinners, and new shoes. Politicians could count on him to bring in the vote, and they in turn gave the ward boss a free hand in pursuing his gambling and liquor businesses.

William Marcy Tweed (1823–1878). Boss of New York City who, through bribes and contract kickbacks, made millions from the city treasury, primarily in the 1860s. "Boss" Tweed was apprehended and later died in jail. Note Thomas Nast's cartoons on the Tweed Ring on p. 480.

Urban Improvements

Streetcars. The electric trolley car changed big city life by expanding the distance a person could live from his work. A "walking city" could not extend more than two and a half miles from its center, whereas the streetcar increased the radius to six miles or more. Frank J. Sprague installed the first practical trolley line in Richmond, Virginia, in 1887–1888.

Bridges. Improved bridge design greatly aided the movement of city dwellers. The most notable was the perfection of the steel cable suspension bridge by *John A. Roebling* who, along with his son, built the Brooklyn Bridge over the East River, connecting Manhattan Island and Brooklyn. The bridge was completed in 1883.

Buildings. Iron-skeleton construction made it possible to build up instead of out, and skyscrapers began to change the city's landscape into a skyline. *Louis Sullivan* was an outstanding architect of the period who designed tall, functional structures.

City Beautiful movement. An effort to redesign cities with an emphasis on large civic centers and broad plazas. Impetus for the movement was provided by Daniel N. Burnham, who built the "White City" for the Chicago World's Fair in 1893 and by Frederick Law Olmsted, the landscape architect who designed New York City's Central Park.

Settlement houses. Neighborhood centers established in slum areas by private individuals or church groups. One of the most famous was *Jane Addams'* Hull House, founded in Chicago in 1889, which boasted a "little theater," a day nursery, and a gymnasium. The settlement houses were often staffed by college students and young professional people who wanted to help bridge the economic and cultural gap.

Religion

1891, *Rerum novarum*. An encyclical issued by Pope Leo XIII in 1890. An encyclical is a letter from the Pope on a specific subject addressed to the hierarchy of the Roman Catholic Church. *Rerum novarum* criticized the excesses of capitalism, defended the right of labor to form unions, and gave approval of some aspects of socialism. It marked a change from the usually conservative Catholic disapproval of organized labor.

Dwight L. Moody (1837–1899). A lay evangelist, that is, one who was not a regular, ordained minister of a particular church, who preached Christianity to the residents of slum areas. The message of this urban missionary was one of God's love and mercy rather than of hell-fire and punishment for sins. Moody did not, however, deal with the practical causes of slum poverty and vice.

Social Gospel. The message of Protestant, that is, non-Roman Catholic Christian, clergymen which focused on trying to improve living conditions rather than on just saving souls. The Social Gospelers advocated child labor legislation, regulation of monopolies, heavy taxes on income and inheritances; in short, they rejected the theory of laissez faire.

Washington Gladden.The most influential preacher of the Social Gospel. In his book *Applied Christianity* (1886) and in other works he defended labor's right to unionize and strike; he supported factory inspection laws; and he advocated strict regulation of public utilities.

Charles M. Sheldon. A Topeka, Kansas, minister whose novel *In His Steps* (1896) reflected the spirit of the Social Gospel and became a best seller. The novel described the mythical city of Raymond, whose citizens asked themselves "What would Jesus do?" before adopting any project. Slum clearance and other social reforms followed.

Social Legislation and Court Interpretation

Legislation. Laws regulating hours and working conditions, women and child labor, met with mixed reactions in the various states, although Congress enacted an eight-hour day for government workers in 1892.

1905, *Lochner* **v.** *New York.* A Supreme Court decision declaring New York's ten-hour act for bakers unconstitutional. The decision was based on the Fourteenth Amendment which forbade the states to "deprive any person of life, liberty or property without due process of law." The Supreme Court said New York was depriving bakers of the liberty of working as long as they wished.

OTHER TERMS TO IDENTIFY

Samuel Gompers (1850–1924). An English immigrant and cigarmaker who helped found the American Federation of Labor in 1886. Except for the year 1895, he was president of the labor organization from 1886 to 1924. Gompers believed in capitalism rather than socialism and felt the union should avoid direct political activity and rely on strikes.

Henry Clay Frick (1849–1919). A coke manufacturer who became general manager of Carnegie Steel Company. Frick brought in strikebreakers to defeat the Homestead strikers and was viewed sympathetically after an anarchist, Alexander Berkman, broke into his office and tried to assassinate him.

Richard Croker (1841–1922). A city boss who ruled Tammany Hall, New York's Democratic political machine, from 1886 to 1902. Croker's machine provided some social and economic favors for the voters, but at the same time he personally accumulated a large fortune.

Henry Ward Beecher (1813–1887). Minister of the Congregationalist Plymouth Church in Brooklyn, New York, who proclaimed that poverty existed in slums because laborers squandered their money on liquor and tobacco. He was the brother of Harriet Beecher Stowe, author of *Uncle Tom's Cabin.*

GLOSSARY

anarchist. A person who believes that all forms of government are oppressive and should be abolished. Many anarchists practice terroristic resistance to the government and those in authority. The organizers of the Haymarket Square demonstration were anarchists.

Beelzebub. The Devil. People opposed to the increasing tide of immigration referred to the newcomers as the "cutthroats of Beelzebub from the Rhine, the Danube, the Vistula and the Elbe," the names referring to rivers running through Germany, Austria, Poland, and other countries of eastern Europe.

capitalism. An economic system which stresses private ownership of the means of production and distribution of products, rather than state control. It is sometimes referred to as free enterprise.

communist. In the 19th century, a person who supported a social system in which there were no classes and in which there was common ownership of the means of production. During the violent railroad strikes of 1877, alarmed citizens began to talk about a revolution triggered by "communist orators."

drone. A male bee which performs no work and produces no honey. Individuals who contribute nothing are referred to as drones. The Knights of Labor used the term for bankers and lawyers.

employers' liability. The responsibility of the owner of a factory, mine, or business to pay a worker's expenses if he or she is injured on the job. The AFL under Gompers demanded employers' liability as part of its legislative goals.

entrepôt. A French word meaning trading or market center or warehouse. New York was the great *entrepôt* for the United States.

geographical mobility. The tendency to move frequently from one geographical location to another.

junto. A small, usually secret group or committee that gathers for some specific aim. The leaders of the 1877 railroad strike were referred to as a junto of men ready to strike down the American way of life.

nativism. An anti-immigrant feeling and a desire to protect the interests of "native" Americans. Nativism was strong in the 1850s and flourished again in the 1880s.

packet lines. Shipping lines that run a regular route, carrying passengers, freight, and mail. Competition between the packet lines such as Cunard, North German Lloyd, and Holland-America drove down the cost of passage for immigrants.

Pinkerton detectives. Private investigators who sometimes worked as spies among labor unions in industrial disputes. They were brought in to protect the strikebreakers in the 1892 Homestead strike. The original Pinkerton agency was started by Allan Pinkerton in Chicago in 1850 and was continued by his sons.

proletariat. Wage earners who make their living from their labor, rather than from investing in a business or factory. They are generally the poorest of the working classes. Urban reformers generally disliked the political bosses in the cities and referred to them as a "proletarian mob" of "illiterate peasants."

pullman. A sleeping car on a railroad. Originally designed and built by George Pullman.

reactionary. A tendency to revert to a former political or social order;

opposing progress and liberalism. In a sense the AFL was a reactionary organization.

scab. A laborer who works while others are on strike; a strikebreaker.

social mobility. The ability in a society to move from one social class to another.

WORDS TO KNOW

Define the following, using the dictionary if necessary.

acculturation   microcosm
assimilate   phalanxes
chimerical   plutocrat
denizens   punctilious
ignominiously   sanguine

SAMPLE QUESTIONS

Multiple Choice

1. Which pair is correctly matched?
   a. Homestead strike: Terence V. Powderly.
   b. Haymarket riot: Samuel Gompers.
   c. Pullman strike: Eugene Debs.
   d. Railroad strike of 1877: Adolph Strasser.
2. Which of the following defended the right of labor to form unions?
   a. *Lochner* v. *New York.*
   b. *Rerum novarum.*
   c. *padrone* system.
   d. *Ritchie* v. *People.*
3. During the latter part of the 19th century the court order known as the *injunction* was most effectively used to:
   a. dissolve trusts.
   b. break strikes.
   c. insure civil liberties for blacks.
   d. assist debtor farmers.
4. Which of the following is *not* correctly matched?
   a. Jane Addams: founder of Hull House.
   b. William Gladden: preacher of the Social Gospel.
   c. Jacob Riis: organizer of the Knights of Labor.
   d. William Marcy Tweed: city boss of New York.
5. The American Protective Association was concerned with:
   a. tariffs.

b. gold
c. anti-Catholic agitation.
d. immigrant aid.

True-False

1. The American Federation of Labor accepted unskilled as well as skilled workers and organized them along industrial lines.
2. The Sherman Antitrust Act was used against the labor union in the Pullman strike.
3. The "new immigrants" of the late 19th century were primarily from Germany and Ireland.
4. The City Beautiful movement established settlement houses.
5. New York's ten-hour work day act for bakers was declared unconstitutional in *Lochner* v. *New York*.

20

Intellectual and Cultural Trends

CHRONOLOGY

1862 Morrill Act
1874 Chautauqua movement originated
1881 Tuskegee Institute founded
1893 Frederick Jackson Turner's "frontier thesis"

CHAPTER CHECKLIST

Education and Information

Tuskegee Institute. Vocational school for blacks founded in Alabama in 1881 by Booker T. Washington. Students were taught to become good farmers and craftsmen; academic subjects were avoided. The Institute reflected the prevailing philosophy of the South: segregation and second-class citizenship for the black.

Calvin M. Woodward. Founder of the Manual Training School in St. Louis, Missouri, in 1880. Woodward thought of vocational training as part of a broad general education rather than as job training for a particular craft. At first industrial leaders supported manual training schools, and consequently labor opposed it, but by 1910 both the AFL and the National Association of Manufacturers were lobbying for more trade schools.

John Dewey (1859–1952). Teacher and philosopher who felt that education ought to build character and teach good citizenship as well as transmit knowledge. He defended his thoeries in *The School and Society* (1899). Dewey taught at the University of Chicago and then at Columbia, stressing his ideas on "learning by doing" and building new information on what the child already knew. His ideas were the basis for what the next generation called "progressive education."

Chautauqua movement. A popular education experience designed to bring a smattering of knowledge on a variety of topics to the masses. The movement originated in 1874 as a summer school for Methodist Sunday School teachers at Lake Chautauqua, New York. It grew into a continuing education program offering lecture series, correspondence courses, and a monthly magazine. The Chautauqua movement reflected a desire for knowledge in an era when formal schooling was still limited for the majority.

Joseph Pulitzer (1847–1911). Newspaper publisher who owned the St. Louis *Post-Dispatch* and the New York *World* and was the first to reach a truly mass audience. In building the *World's* circulation to over 1 million copies daily, he used techniques whch are sometimes described as "yellow journalism": human interest stories involving scandal and crime, sensational exposés, and crusades against corruption. Pulitzer later established the Pulitzer prizes which are still awarded annually for achievements in various aspects of literature. Note the portrait of Pulitzer on p. 494.

Edward Bok (1863–1930). Editor of the *Ladies' Home Journal* from 1889 and a pioneer in popular journalism. Under Bok, the *Journal* combined articles on child care and gardening with serious contributions by outstanding novelists and political leaders. He did not merely cater to public tastes, but created new tastes, and was highly successful in the new field of mass-circulation magazines.

Charles Eliot (1834–1926). President of Harvard University in Massachusetts from 1869 to 1909. He transformed the school by introducing the elective system, that is, eliminating the long list of required courses, and adding a number of new offerings such as modern languages and laboratory sciences. He brought in new faculty and encouraged them to use new teaching methods.

Johns Hopkins University. A university founded in Maryland in 1876 by Johns Hopkins, who had made his fortune with the Baltimore and Ohio Railroad. The school specialized in graduate education; that is, it emphasized research and making a contribution to knowledge. The first president was Daniel Coit Gilman, who modeled the school on German universities, where meticulous scholarly research was stressed.

University of Chicago. A university founded in Illinois in 1892 and funded by John D. Rockefeller. The first president, William Rainey Harper, raided the faculties of other schools by offering high salaries and academic freedom and patterned the school after Johns Hopkins.

1862, Morrill Act. Congressional act providing aid to states for higher education. The act granted land to each state at a rate of 30,000 acres for each senator and representative. The land-grant universities which were established, such as the University of Illinois and Michigan State, were open to new ideas. They were usually co-educational and offered a wide variety of courses.

Scholars

Josiah Willard Gibbs (1839–1903). Professor of mathematical physics at Yale from 1871 to 1903. He created an entirely new science, physical chemistry. Although his theories were little understood at the time, Gibbs' ideas led eventually to advances in metallurgy and in the manufacture of plastic and drugs.

Lester Frank Ward (1841–1913). Sociologist whose important work was *Dynamic Sociology* (1883). Ward opposed the laissez faire, Social Darwinist ideas of the time. He felt that government should regulate the economy and that society would evolve through careful social planning. Ward help lay the theoretical basis for the modern welfare state.

Oliver Wendell Holmes, Jr. (1841–1935). Judge who served on the Massachusetts Supreme Court for almost 20 years and on the United States Supreme Court from 1902 to 1931. In *The Common Law* (1881) and in court decisions he expressed the view that interpretation of laws should evolve as times and conditions changed.

Frederick Jackson Turner (1861–1932). Historian whose address before the American Historical Society in 1893 entitled "The Significance of the Frontier in American History" opened new insights into the history of the West. Turner argued that the characteristics which made Americans different from Europeans could be traced to the frontier experience through which every section of the country had passed. It had made Americans individualistic and their society democratic. Turner's work was important because it pointed out the need to investigate the evolution of institutions and encouraged historians to concentrate on social and economic as well as political topics. Turner was a professor of history at Wisconsin (1885–1910) and at Harvard (1910–1924).

Literature

Age of Realism. A trend away from the sentimental romanticism of the previous generation. By the 1880s realism began to emerge both in art and in literature. Novelists wrote about current social problems and created characters of every social class.

"Local color" school. Writers who turned to the regions they knew best for material. They reflected the new realism in their concern for exact description and their fascination with local types. An example was the "Uncle Remus" stories of Joel Chandler Harris.

Mark Twain (1835–1910). Pen name of Samuel L. Clemens. Twain grew up in Missouri on the banks of the Mississippi and worked briefly as a riverboat pilot. His pseudonym is the river call for a water depth of two fathoms, "mark twain." Twain wrote with humor and insight about typical American scenes, as in *The Gilded Age* (1873) and *Tom Sawyer* (1876). *Huckleberry Finn* (1884) is considered his masterpiece.

William Dean Howells (1837–1920). Editor of the *Atlantic Monthly* and then of *Harper's,* who was a prolific critic and novelist. He was a champion of realism, and his works displayed a concern with social problems. Several of his important novels were *The Rise of Silas Lapham* (1885), which dealt with the ethical conflicts faced by businessmen, and *A Hazard of New Fortunes* (1890), which attempted to portray the range of metropolitan life in New York.

Henry James (1843–1916). American author who spent most of his life in Europe. The major theme of his works was the clash of American and European cultures, and he was particularly interested in the interaction of wealthy, sensitive people with their environment. Two of his more important novels were *The American* (1877) and *The Portrait of a Lady* (1881).

Art

Thomas Eakins (1844–1916). Artist whose works reflected the spirit of realism. After studying in Europe, he spent the rest of his life teaching at the Academy of Fine Arts in Philadelphia. His interest in realism and the scientific spirit can be seen in his mastery of human anatomy as evidenced in *The Gross Clinic* (1875), illustrating a surgical operation, and in *The Swimming Hole* (1883). See this painting on p. 506.

Winslow Homer (1836–1910). Realist painter who was best known for his watercolors. He had an intense concern for accuracy and in some ways resembled the local colorists of American literature. Like them, he used romantic elements in his work, such as the violence and drama of raw nature as seen in the *Fox Hunt* (1893).

James A. McNeill Whistler (1834–1903). American painter who spent most of his life in Europe. Some of his works were realistic while others were romantic in spirit. His most famous painting, *Arrangement in Grey and Black,* is better known as "Whistler's Mother."

Pragmatic Approach

Pragmatism. A philosophical concept of the late 19th century which was first expressed by Charles Peirce and developed by William James. Pragmatism denied the existence of absolute truth and seemed to imply that the end justified the means, that what worked was more important than what ought to be. The pragmatic approach inspired a reform spirit.

Evolution. The theory of Charles Darwin that plants and animals had their origin in previously existing species which changed and developed through the generations. This idea, expressed in Darwin's *Origin of the Species* (1859), contradicted the story of the creation as presented in the book of Genesis in the Bible and caused much controversy. Darwin's theory of evolution contributed to the pragmatic approach in that fixed ideas and eternal truths made little sense in a world that was constantly evolving.

William James (1842–1910). Physician, psychologist, and philosopher who developed the ideas of pragmatism. He felt that truth was relative; it did not exist in the abstract. He is considered the father of modern psychology, and his book *Principles of Psychology* (1890) was used as a standard textbook for years. Note the picture of James on p. 509.

OTHER TERMS TO IDENTIFY

Thorstein Veblen (1857–1929). Economist and social theorist who criticized the great influence of big business in America. In *The Higher Learning in America* (1918) Veblen stated that "the intrusion of businesslike ideals, aims, and methods" harmed the universities. Schools became overly concerned with enrolling more and more students and with stressing the practical rather than the humanistic values of education.

"Institutional school" of economics. A group of economists who did on-the-spot studies of sweatshops, factories, and mines, feeling that the method would lead both to theoretical understanding and to practical social reform and government regulation.

Herbert Spencer (1820–1903). English philosopher and evolutionist who rejected the idea of any government interference in business or society. The most fit would survive. This application of Charles Darwin's theories to society was known as Social Darwinism.

***Congressional Government* (1885).** The doctoral dissertation of Woodrow Wilson at Johns Hopkins. Wilson concluded that real authority lay in the committees of Congress, which had no constitutional basis at all. His work was significant because it dealt with the actual workings of government rather than with abstract principles.

Naturalism. A literary trend which went beyond realism. Its followers often wrote about the dark side of life. They were Darwinists who felt that man was essentially a helpless creature whose fate was determined by his environment. An outstanding example of a naturalist was Stephen Crane, who used settings such as the slums in *Maggie, A Girl of the Streets* (1893) and Civil War battles in *The Red Badge of Courage* (1895).

Albert Pinkham Ryder (1847–1917). A romantic painter who spent his adult years in New York City painting in an attic studio. He typified the solitary romantic—brooding, eccentric, mystical—and painted unusual canvases such as *The Race Track*.

Mary Cassatt (1845–1926). An American artist who settled permanently in Paris and became part of the French impressionist movement.

Charles Peirce (1839–1914). An original thinker who is considered the founder of pragmatism. He argued that concepts could only be understood in terms of their practical effects. When one accepted the truth of evolution, logic required that one accept the impermanence even of scientific laws.

GLOSSARY

case method. Technique used at Harvard Law School, among others, in which course material is based on actual cases rather than on abstract principles.

eternal verities. Statements, principles, or beliefs considered to be established and permanent truth. If one believed that evolution were constantly taking place, fixed systems and eternal verities were difficult to justify in the world.

journeyman. One who has served his apprenticeship and is a qualified worker. The day of the journeyman printer-editor was over by the late 1800s, and magazine and newspaper publishing was becoming big business.

nom de plume. The French phrase for pen name; a pseudonym adopted by a writer. Mark Twain was the *nom de plume* of Samuel Clemens.

patent medicine. A drug or medical preparation that is protected by a patent and can be bought without a prescription. In the 19th century many patent medicines were home brewed, peddled by traveling salesmen, and their primary ingredient was alcohol. Edward Bok showed his disapproval of these medicines for which fantastic claims were made by refusing to accept patent medicine advertisements in the *Ladies' Home Journal*.

probate court. A court of law which establishes the validity of a will and administers the estate of one who has died. While the estate of Leland Stanford was tied up in probate court, his widow paid Stanford University professors out of her allowance for household expenses.

syndicated article. A newspaper article or column which is published simultaneously in newspapers throughout the country.

three R's. Reading, 'riting, and 'rithmetic. Traditionally, American teachers had emphasized the three R's, but new educational methods and ideas emerged in the late 19th century.

WORDS TO KNOW
Define the following, using the dictionary if necessary.

assiduity	mountebank
circumlocution	mutability
consanguinity	pedagogues
execrable	perfidious
lacrymose	quaff

SAMPLE QUESTIONS

Multiple Choice
1. Huckleberry Finn:
   a. Samuel Clemens' pen name.

    b. a local color writer.
    c. a novel by Mark Twain.
    d. Tom Sawyer's brother.
2. The person who introduced the "elective system" into higher education was:
    a. T. S. Eliot.
    b. Edward Bok.
    c. Charles Eliot.
    d. William Rainey.
3. The significance of the frontier in the development of American institutions was pointed out by:
    a. S. A. Maverick.
    b. Frederick Jackson Turner.
    c. Josiah Willard Gibbs.
    d. Henry Carter Adams.
4. The Chautauqua movement:
    a. a continuing education program.
    b. a group of artists whose works reflected realism.
    c. the "local color" novelists in New York.
    d. an interpretation of Darwin's theory of evolution.
5. A philosophy which denied the existence of absolute truth and was developed by William James:
    a. naturalism.
    b. realism.
    c. impressionism.
    d. pragmatism.

Matching

1. ____Thomas Eakins

2. ____William Dean Howells

3. ____Henry James

4. ____Edward Bok

5. ____Joseph Pulitzer

6. ____John Dewey

7. ____Ottmar Mergenthaler

a. developed the linotype machine.

b. sociologist who felt that the government should regulate the economy.

c. educator and philosopher with progressive ideas about education.

d. newspaper editor who used "yellow journalism" techniques.

e. author who wrote on the clash of American and European cultures.

f. a realistic painter who was interested in human anatomy.

g. Supreme Court Justice who felt laws should evolve as conditions changed.

8.____ William James

h. editor of the *Atlantic Monthly* and *Harpers* who was a champion of realism.

9.____ Oliver Wendell Holmes

i. editor of *Ladies' Home Journal*.

10.____ Lester Frank Ward

j. philosopher and psychologist who developed the ideas of pragmatism.

ANSWERS

Multiple Choice: c, c, b, a, d. Matching: f, h, e, i, d, c, a, j, g, b.

21

National Politics 1877-1896

CHRONOLOGY

1870s Granger movement
1880s Alliance movement
1881   Assassination of President Garfield
1883   Pendleton Act
1894   Coxey's march on Washington, D.C.
1896   Bryan's "cross of gold" speech

CHAPTER CHECKLIST

Issues

"Waving the bloody shirt." The practice of politicians reminding the voters of the North that most of the southerners who had seceded from the Union and fought in the Civil War were Democrats. To vote for a Democrat was to vote for the party of disloyalty.

   Black rights. The Republicans waved the bloody shirt and warned southern blacks that they had better vote Republican if they wanted to hold on to their new freedoms.

   Veterans' pensions. Politicians waved the bloody shirt to get the vote of Union veterans, but in return the veterans wanted pensions. Their goals were pushed by the *Grand Army of the Republic,* an organization which first demanded aid for veterans with service-connected disabilities, then for those with any disability, and eventually for all former Union soldiers.

Tariff. A tax on imports. Manufacturers wanted high tariffs so their products could undersell foreign competitors. The American product might in reality be more expensive because of the cost of new factories

RUTHERFORD BIRCHARD HAYES (1822–1893), 19th President

Born in Ohio; graduated from Kenyon College and Harvard Law
   School.
General in the Union Army during the Civil War.
Republican member of the House of Representatives (1865–1867).
Governor of Ohio (1867–1871, 1875–1877).
President (1877–1881) after a close and disputed race with Samuel Til-
   den.

JAMES ABRAM GARFIELD (1831–1881), 20th President

Born in Ohio and graduated from Williams College.
General in the Union Army during the Civil War.
Republican member of the House of Representatives (1863–1880).
President (1881).
Shot by Charles Guiteau, a disappointed office seeker, on July 2, 1881,
   and died on September 19.

and higher wages for labor, but the tax added to the foreign product made
the latter more expensive for the American consumer. Both parties believed in protective tariffs, although the Democrats professed to believe in
moderation. However, each time tariff rates came up in Congress, congressmen voted for high rates for industries in their own districts.

Currency reform. The rapid growth of population and economic activity
increased the need for currency in circulation. Yet many people felt the
government should withdraw the *greenbacks,* paper money issued during
the Civil War which could not be converted into gold or silver. The National Greenback party favored keeping paper currency and ran an unsuccessful presidential candidate in 1876. The two major parties were split
internally on the issue and therefore did not face it. The Republicans professed to be the party of sound money, although most western Republicans wanted inflation. Within the Democratic party the conservative, or
"Bourbon," Democrats also wanted sound money or deflation.

Civil service reform. Government jobs were filled by political appoin-
tees, but it became apparent that some measure of permanent, professional administration was needed. Both parties wrote civil service planks
into their platforms, but neither really wanted to give up its political patronage. A start was made with the 1883 *Pendleton Act* which "classified"
about 10 percent of all government jobs and created a bipartisan Civil

Service Commission to prepare and administer competitive examinations for these positions. The act made it illegal to force officeholders to make political contributions and empowered the president to extend the list of jobs under Civil Service. Today a large percentage of government jobs is under Civil Service rather than appointed by the president.

Congressional Leaders

James Gillespie Blaine (1830–1893). A Republican who served in the state legislature of Maine, in the House of Representatives, and in the Senate, where he was leader of the Half-Breed faction of the Republican party. He was secretary of state under Garfield and again under Benjamin Harrison. Blaine was the unsuccessful Republican candidate for president in the 1884 election. Concerning the issues, he favored sound currency

---

CHESTER ALAN ARTHUR (1829–1886), 21st President

Born in Vermont and graduated from Union College.
Studied law and entered politics in New York, where he became part of
the Stalwart faction of the Republican party.
Customs collector of New York (1881–1887).
Vice-president under James Garfield (1881).
President (1881–1885) as a result of Garfield's assassination.

GROVER CLEVELAND (1837–1908), 22nd and 24th President

Born in New York and through self-education became an attorney.
Democratic mayor of Buffalo and governor of New York.
President for two terms (1885–1889, 1893–1897). He also won the
largest popular vote in the election of 1888, but lost in the electoral
college to Harrison.

BENJAMIN HARRISON (1883–1901), 23rd President

Born in Ohio, the grandson of President William Henry Harrison
(1841).
Moved to Indiana and practiced law.
General in the Union Army during the Civil War.
Republican senator from Indiana (1881–1887).
President (1889–1893).

and a protective tariff. Blaine was also interested in foreign affairs, particularly those involving Latin America.

Roscoe Conkling (1829–1888). New York politician and leader of the Stalwart faction of the Republican party. He served in the House and then in the Senate almost continuously from 1859–1881, and resigned in that year because of a patronage feud with Garfield, who leaned toward the Halfbreeds.

John Sherman (1823–1900). A Republican member of Congress from 1855 to 1898, who was sometimes called the "Ohio Icicle" because of his stiff personality. Sherman had a reputation for expertise in financial matters, and gave his name to the 1890 Sherman Antitrust Act.

Thomas B. Reed (1839–1902). An ultraconservative Republican congressman from Maine who was elected speaker of the House in 1890. His autocratic methods of speeding up business won him the nickname "Czar" Reed.

Richard P. Bland (1835–1899). A Democrat from Missouri who was a congressman from 1873 to 1899, except for 1895–1897. "Silver Dick" Bland spent most of his political energies fighting for the free coinage of silver.

Benjamin Butler (1818–1893). A Massachusetts politician who frequently changed his party hat. He was a states' rights Democrat before the war and became a Radical Republican congressman during Reconstruction. In 1878 he was elected to Congress as a Greenbacker, and in 1882 he became governor of Massachusetts as a Democrat. Butler favored currency inflation and was concerned with the interests of the laboring man.

The Farmer and Politics

1870s, Granger movement. A farmers' organization which flourished in the West and South. Its members were politically active and pushed Granger laws through state legislatures to regulate the railroads and grain elevators.

1880s, Alliance movement. Local farmers' clubs which organized first at the state level and then on a regional basis. These organizations adopted somewhat differing policies but agreed that agricultural prices were too low, that transportation costs were too high, and that something was wrong with the nation's financial system. Alliance members were involved in politics at the local and state levels.

1890s, Populist movement. An association of Alliance members, Knights of Labor leaders, and various reformers who decided to create a new national party. In February 1892, 800 met at St. Louis, organized the People's party, and called for a national convention to meet in Omaha, Nebraska, in July, where they nominated General James Weaver of Iowa as their presidential candidate. The Omaha Platform set forth the major goals of the Populist party:

Graduated income tax, that is, people with more money should pay a greater proportion of their income in taxes.

National ownership of railroads, telegraph, and telephone systems.

"Subtreasury" plan that would permit farmers to store nonperishable crops in warehouses and borrow money from the government, using the crops as security. When the price of the produce went up, the farmer could sell his crop, pay off his debt, and hopefully make a profit.

Unlimited coinage of silver and an increase in the money supply.

Adoption of the initiative and the referendum.

Election of United States senators by popular vote rather than by the state legislatures.

Eight-hour work day.

Restriction of "undesirable" immigration.

The Currency Conflict

Bimetallic standard. Currency in the United States was traditionally based on both gold and silver. Their market value fluctuated according to the supply of the two metals, but the ratio at which the government issued currency was set by law.

Coinage Act of 1873. Demonetized silver. No one had been selling silver to the Mint for coinage because the government had underpriced it and people preferred to sell it on the open market. But in 1874 the market price of silver went down, and people who wanted to sell to the government could not. Consequently they called the act the "Crime of 1873."

1878, Bland-Allison Act. An act which authorized the purchase of $2–4 million of silver a month at the market price. This measure did not significantly put more money in circulation because the government purchased only the minimum amount.

1890, Sherman Silver Purchase Act. An act which required the government to buy 4.5 million ounces of silver monthly; repealed in 1893.

1894, Coxey's Army. A group of unemployed workers, led by an Ohio businessman, Jacob Coxey, who marched to Washington, D.C., to dramatize their plight, caused by the Panic of 1893. Coxey wanted the government to undertake a federal public works program in which local communities would be authorized to exchange noninterest-bearing bonds with the Treasury for $500 million in paper money. The funds would be used to hire the unemployed to build roads. Coxey argued that this scheme would pump money into the economy, provide work for the jobless, and benefit the nation by improving transportation.

About 500 demonstrators reached the Capitol grounds where Coxey and two other leaders were arrested for stepping on the grass and the others were dispersed. Coxey's plans were dismissed as being too radical. It was not until the New Deal of the 1930s that such federal works programs were implemented.

Election of 1896

Republican: William McKinley. His campaign, which stressed allegiance to the gold standard, was run by *Marcus Alonzo Hanna,* a "kingmaker" who felt that money was the key to political power and demanded millions from Republican businessmen across the country. McKinley conducted a *front-porch campaign,* remaining at his Ohio home and receiving visiting delegations from all sectors. Note the picture on p. 534.

Democratic: William Jennings Bryan. Bryan's "cross of gold" speech at the Democratic convention helped sway the platform toward the unlimited coinage of silver at the ratio of 16:1, and it also helped win him the nomination. His speech was for silver against gold, for western farmers against the industrial East, and closed with the declaration, "You shall not crucify mankind upon a cross of gold!" Bryan conducted an energetic handshaking, speech-making campaign all over the country, hammering away at the money issue. See the picture of Bryan on p. 532.

Populist: William Jennings Bryan. Since Bryan had expressed many Populist sentiments, the party nominated him for the presidency although it selected a different vice-presidential candidate, Tom Watson. The Populists were particularly pleased with Bryan's advocating the unlimited coinage of silver. Although many Populists were afraid that supporting the Democratic candidate would cause them to lose their identity, they feared that to vote otherwise would assure victory to McKinley.

National Democratic: John M. Palmer. The extreme gold bugs of the Democratic party nominated the 79-year-old Palmer to draw votes away from Bryan.

The Republican, McKinley, won the election. See the map entitled "The Election of 1896" on p. 536.

OTHER TERMS TO IDENTIFY

"Bourbon" Democrats. Conservative southern Democrats who refused to accept the results of the Civil War. Like the Bourbons, the French ruling family, they "learned nothing and forgot nothing." The Bourbons lost their throne and later regained it, yet continued to make the same mistakes. Southern Democrats lost political control during Reconstruction.

Stalwarts and Half-Breeds. Two factions within the Republican party in the 1880s. The Stalwarts, led by Senator Roscoe Conkling of New York, believed in the spoils system and were opposed to civil service reform. The Half-Breeds supposedly believed in moderate reform, but most were not sincere. Actually, their chief reason for existence was to obtain as many government jobs for members of their faction as possible.

Charles Guiteau. The lawyer who shot President Garfield in the Washington railroad station in July 1881 and who, although evidently insane, was hanged. Guiteau, a Stalwart, had been unsuccessful in seeking a government job and felt that he had not obtained one because Garfield was favoring the Half-Breeds. After shooting Garfield, Guiteau cried, "I am a Stalwart, and Arthur is president now." Vice-president Chester Arthur was a Stalwart.

Mulligan letters. A group of letters which showed James G. Blaine in a bad light and was used against him in the campaign of 1884. In 1876 a House investigating committee, on the testimony of James Mulligan, charged Blaine with using his influence to aid the Little Rock and Fort Smith Railroad. The Mulligan letters, written by Blaine to a Boston businessman, were in the possession of Mulligan until Blaine got them away from him and then refused to surrender them. The letters contained compromising evidence, and at the bottom of one was Blaine's demand, "Burn this letter."

Mugwumps. Reform Republicans who refused to support Blaine in the 1884 election and voted instead for the Democrat Cleveland. The term "mugwump" was derived from an Algonquin Indian word meaning "big chief," and it implied that the Mugwumps felt they were above party loyalty.

Murchison letter. A letter published during the 1888 election which cost the Democrats a number of votes. It was supposedly written by "Charles Murchison" but actually was authored by a California Republican, George Osgoodby, and sent to Sir Lionel Sackville-West, the British minister in Washington, asking his advice as to which candidate he should vote for. Sackville-West intimated that Cleveland would best serve the interests of Great Britain, whereupon the Republicans published the letter. As a result many Irish-Americans, who were traditionally anti-British, voted for Cleveland's opponent, Harrison.

Tom Watson (1856–1922). Georgia politician and author who was active in the Alliance movement and then in the Populist party. Watson was the Populists' vice-presidential candidate in 1896 and their presidential candidate in 1904.

Ignatius Donnelly (1831–1901). Minnesota politician who was a leader in liberal third-party movements. He helped organize the Grange movement in the 1870s and helped form the Populist party and ran as its presidential candidate in 1900. Donnelly also authored a number of books, including the novels *Atlantis* (1882) and *Caesar's Column* (1891).

1895, *Pollock* v. *Farmers' Loan and Trust Company*. A Supreme Court decision which invalidated the provision in the 1894 Wilson-Gorman Tariff Act that placed a 2 percent tax on personal incomes above $4000. The Court felt that a federal income tax was unconstitutional. This decision led to a proposal to amend the Constitution which was accomplished by the Sixteenth Amendment in 1913, allowing federal income taxes.

GLOSSARY

ad valorem. A Latin phrase meaning "in proportion to the value." Tariff duties after the Civil War rose to an average of 50 percent ad valorem.

commonwealth. A nation or state governed by the people. In 1888 the British historian and statesman, James Bryce, published *The American Commonwealth* in which he described American politicians as clinging to outworn issues.

czar. The title formerly used for the king or emperor of Russia. Sometimes spelled tsar. The term is also used to refer to one in authority who acts like a tyrant. Speaker of the House Thomas Reed was nicknamed "Czar" because of his autocratic way of conducting business.

graduated income tax. An annual tax on one's income, the higher the income, the higher the percentage. For example, a single person would pay a 19 percent tax on a $6000 income, whereas he or she would pay 34 percent of a $20,000 income.

initiative. A method which enables voters to initiate bills in the state legislature. By obtaining a certain percentage of the voters' signatures on a petition, citizens can force the legislature to at least bring up a desired law and vote on it. The Populist party platform of 1892 advocated the initiative as a method of making government more responsive to the needs of the people. The initative still exists in some states but was never enacted at the national level.

logrolling. Trading votes among legislators to achieve passage of laws of interest to one another. A good deal of logrolling occurred in Congress every time a new tariff bill came up, for legislators wanted the highest possible duties to protect industries in their own districts.

patronage. The power or action of appointing supporters to governmental or political positions. Opponents to civil service reform vowed that patronage was the lifeblood of politics. People expected to be rewarded with a job for helping the candidate win.

pentecost. A religious holiday. According to Acts 2 in the Bible, on the Pentecost after the resurrection of Jesus, the Holy Ghost descended on his disciples. Tongues resembling fire came over them, and they spoke in different languages. In 1890 farmers' groups actively entered politics with a religious fervor, and in Kansas, according to one chronicler, it was "a pentecost of politics in which a tongue of flame sat upon every man, and each spake as the spirit gave him utterance."

pork-barrel legislation. A government act benefiting a particular locale, such as building a dam or improving a harbor. During the late 19th century, congressmen became overly concerned with passing pork-barrel legislation which would win them favor with their own constituents rather than concentrating on issues of national importance. In order to pass these local projects through Congress, a good deal of logrolling went on.

reciprocity agreement. A commercial policy or trade agreement between two or more nations designed to increase trade, generally by mutually lowering certain tariffs. Most of the time James Blaine supported the protective system, but he also advocated reciprocity agreements to increase trade.

referendum. The submission of an actual or proposed law to a direct vote of the people for their approval or rejection. The Populist platform of 1892 supported the referendum and viewed it as a "people's veto" of legislation. A number of states have the referendum, but it does not exist at the national level.

status quo. A Latin phrase meaning "the existing condition of things as they are at the present." The election of 1896 was not a triumph of the status quo, but marked the coming of age of modern America.

tenure. A period of holding an office or occupation. The source of the Senate's influence lay in the long tenure of some of its members, which enabled them to master the craft of politics.

Tweedledum and Tweedledee. Two persons resembling one another so closely that they are indistinguishable. The phrase was coined by John Byrom in his satire *On the Feuds Between Handel and Bononcini,* about two rival musicians in the 18th century. Tweedledum and Tweedledee were also characters in *Alice's Adventures in Wonderland.* In the late 19th century, the party platforms were so similar that the voters had to choose, essentially, between Tweedledum and Tweedledee.

white-collar worker. A worker, either salaried or professional, whose work usually does not involve manual labor and who is expected to dress with some degree of formality. White-collar workers, as well as farmers, laborers, and shopkeepers, evenly distributed their votes between the Democrats and the Republicans.

writ of habeas corpus. A written court order designed to bring a jailed person before a court or judge to determine if he is being unlawfully held or should be released. The Supreme Court denied a writ of habeas corpus to Eugene Debs, who had been imprisoned for disobeying a federal injunction during the Pullman strike.

WORDS TO KNOW

Define the following, using the dictionary if necessary.

abstemious	chameleon
abysmal	mien
acrimonious	nefarious
apothecary	nostrums
aquiline	perennial

SAMPLE QUESTIONS

Multiple Choice

1. The assassination of James Garfield led to the:
   a. repeal of the Sherman Silver Purchase Act.
   b. Tenure of Office Act.
   c. Pendleton Act.
   d. Bland-Allison Act.
2. The Greenback party was devoted to securing:
   a. a gold standard.
   b. a silver standard.
   c. an inflated paper currency.
   d. a retirement of greenbacks from circulation.
3. Who of the following led a march on Washington to get the government to undertake a federal public works program?
   a. Jacob Coxey.
   b. James G. Blaine.
   c. Benjamin Butler.
   d. John Sherman.
4. Which of the following was *not* part of the Populist platform of 1892?
   a. the subtreasury plan.
   b. the initiative and the referendum.
   c. government ownership of railroads.
   d. civil service reform.
5. The "cross of gold" speech advocated:
   a. a higher tariff.
   b. the unlimited coinage of silver.
   c. a religious revival.
   d. a public works program in the cities.

True-False

1. The Grand Army of the Republic was composed of Union veterans who lobbied for veterans' pensions.
2. Roscoe Conkling was leader of the Half-Breed faction of the Republican party.
3. Sound money men supported greenbacks and unlimited coinage of silver.
4. Even though the silverites lost the 1896 election, new discoveries of gold in Alaska and South Africa soon led to an expansion of the money supply.
5. Both political parties, in practice, supported a protective tariff.

ANSWERS
Multiple Choice: c, c, a, d, b. True-False: T, F, F, T, T.

22

From Isolation to Empire

CHRONOLOGY

1867	Purchase of Alaska
1898	Sinking of the *Maine*
1898	Spanish-American War
1898	Annexation of Hawaii
1898	Treaty of Paris with Spain
1899, 1900	Open Door notes
1903	Hay–Bunau-Varilla Treaty
1904	Roosevelt Corollary to Monroe Doctrine

CHAPTER CHECKLIST

Isolation or Expansion

Isolation. United States foreign policy toward Europe. A disdain for Europeans was based on several factors:

Unique civilization. Americans were proud of themselves and considered Europeans aristocratic and decadent.

War memories. Bitter memories from the Revolution; the Napoleonic Wars, which included the War of 1812; and the Civil War, when some powers had seemed sympathetic toward the Confederacy, remained.

Distance. The Atlantic Ocean made isolation practical: It was hard to launch an attack or be attacked across it.

Expansion. United States foreign policy in the Caribbean and across the Pacific Ocean. Expansionism developed gradually between 1860 and 1900 for a number of reasons:

Foreign trade. Agricultural and industrial goods were being produced and exported at an ever increasing rate. As industrialists competed in foreign markets, they became interested in world affairs. See the chart "American Foreign Trade, 1870–1914" on p. 541.

Intellectual currents. Darwin's theories of survival of the fittest were applied to international affairs. Josiah Strong, in *Our Country* (1885), stated that the Anglo-Saxon race, meaning Americans and British, had a genius for colonization and that American civilization would move into other cultures and be the survivor.

European example. European powers were already colonizing Africa and Asia to their economic advantage, and some Americans felt the United States should do likewise.

Military strategy. Overseas bases would be necessary if the United States were ever to build and maintain a powerful navy.

Captain Alfred Thayer Mahan (1840–1914). A naval captain whose theories on the importance of sea power were expounded in *The Influence of Sea Power Upon History* (1890) and *The Influence of Sea Power Upon the French Revolution and Empire* (1892). Mahan applied his theories to the American scene, stating that in addition to building a modern naval fleet, the United States should acquire coaling stations and bases in the Caribbean Sea, annex the Hawaiian Islands, and cut a canal across Central America. His influential disciples included Henry Cabot Lodge.

Foreign Involvement

Hawaii

1875. Reciprocity treaty admitted Hawaiian sugar to the United States duty free in return for a promise not to yield any territory to a foreign power.

1887. United States obtained the right to establish a naval base at Pearl Harbor.

1890. McKinley Tariff Act discontinued the duty on raw sugar from all countries and compensated American producers of cane and beet sugar by granting them a bounty of two cents a pound. This action destroyed the advantage the Hawaiians had gained in the reciprocity treaty, and the price of Hawaiian sugar fell drastically.

1891. Queen Liliuokalani, a nationalist who wanted "Hawaii for the Hawaiians" and an end to foreign interference, ascended the throne.

1893. Americans staged an insurrection, overthrew Queen Liliuokalani, and set up a provisional government which was promptly recognized by the United States minister, John L. Stevens. The new government negotiated a treaty of annexation with the United States which was withdrawn by the isolationist President Cleveland when he took office.

1894. An independent Republic of Hawaii was established.

1897. When McKinley became president, a new treaty of annexation was negotiated, but it failed to be ratified by the Senate.

1898. Congress annexed the Hawaiian Islands by joint resolution, a procedure which requires a majority vote in both houses.

1959. Hawaii entered the Union as the 50th state.

1889, Pan-American Conference. A gathering arranged by Secretary of State James G. Blaine convening in Washington to discuss hemispheric problems. The Latin American delegates were fearful of the United States' designs, and the only accomplishment was the establishment of an International Bureau later known as the Pan-American Union to promote commercial and cultural exchange. The conference was significant because it marked the first effort by the United States to assume the leadership of the nations of the hemisphere.

1891, *Baltimore* incident in Chile. Some sailors from the U.S.S. *Baltimore* on shore leave in Chile were attacked by a mob. Two were killed, a dozen were injured, and President Harrison demanded an apology and reparations. When Chile was slow in its response, Harrison sent virtually a war message to Congress. Chile then offered a formal apology and agreed to pay damages, but Pan-American goodwill was damaged.

1895, Venezuela-British Guiana boundary dispute. A conflict concerning the correct border of the independent country of Venezuela and the English colony of British Guiana, which is now independent Guyana. Secretary of State Richard Olney insisted that the United States be allowed to arbitrate the dispute, for he feared that the British would send in troops to take over a good portion of Venezuela. This action would be contrary to the Monroe Doctrine, a cornerstone of American hemispheric foreign policy although not recognized under international law. After much "saber-rattling" by President Cleveland, Great Britain agreed to let a United States commission settle the boundary problem, and subsequently, Britain received most of the area. The outcome of the incident was significant because it marked the beginning of an era of Anglo-American friendship. At the same time, however, it made another Latin American country question the value of United States intervention.

WILLIAM McKINLEY (1843–1901), 25th President

Born in Ohio and the last Civil War veteran to become president.

Republican member of the House of Representatives for 12 years. The tariff was his particular interest.

Governor of Ohio (1891–1895).

President (1897–1901).

Shot by an anarchist, Leon Czolgosz, on September 6 and died on September 14, 1901. He was succeeded by Vice-president Theodore Roosevelt.

Spanish-American War

STEPS LEADING TO UNITED STATES INVOLVEMENT

"Butcher" Weyler's reconcentration camps. Compounds in Cuba where civilians were herded so they could not aid the revolutionaries living off the land. They were set up by the Spanish general, Valeriano Weyler. News of the bad conditions in these camps, lack of food and shelter and a high disease rate, got back to the United States, causing indignation among humanitarians who wanted United States intervention.

New York *Journal* vs. New York *World*. Newspaper competition to increase circulation caused the papers to keep alive resentment of Spanish colonial policies in Cuba. The leaders in this campaign were Joseph Pulitzer's New York *World* and William Randolph Hearst's New York *Journal*.

Deputy de Lôme Letter. A letter from the Spanish minister in Washington, Deputy de Lôme, to a friend in Cuba, which was stolen and published in Hearst's *Journal*. The letter contained insults to President McKinley and stirred public outrage.

Sinking of the *Maine*. On February 15, 1898, the battleship *Maine,* in Havana harbor to protect American lives and property if necessary, exploded, killing 260 crew members. American interventionists jumped to the conclusion that Spain had planted the submarine mine, or underwater explosive device, although Spain was desperately trying to keep the United States from intervening. Nonetheless, "Remember the *Maine*" became a battle cry for those wanting war.

April 20, 1898. Congress passed a joint resolution recognizing the independence of Cuba and authorizing the use of armed forces to drive out the Spanish. The *Teller Amendment* stated that the United States had no intention of annexing Cuba.

The War in the Philippines

Commodore George Dewey (1837–1917). Naval commander who destroyed the Spanish fleet at Manila harbor on May 1, 1898. It was not until August 13, however, that reinforcements arrived to capture Manila.

Emilio Aguinaldo (1869–1964). A Filipino nationalist who established contact with Dewey and with his irregulars helped capture Manila. When Aguinaldo later realized that the Philippines were not going to become independent, he led a guerrilla war against the American occupation forces.

The War in Cuba and Puerto Rico

A blockade of the Spanish fleet in Santiago harbor and then its destruction, plus battles on Cuba such as the storming of San Juan Hill near Santiago, caused a rapid surrender by the Spanish in July. Note the map entitled "The Spanish-American War in the Caribbean, 1898" on p. 551.

Puerto Rico was quickly occupied by United States troops.

August 12, 1898. Armistice signed.

1898, Treaty of Paris. The treaty formally ending the Spanish-American War was signed in Paris on December 10, 1898, and ratified by the necessary two-thirds vote in the Senate on February 6, 1899. Cuba became independent, and Puerto Rico, the island of Guam in the Pacific, and the Philippines became United States territories. The United States paid $20 million for the Philippines.

Colonialism and Its Opponents

Opponents to colonies. Some people felt that the United States was betraying its heritage by acquiring new territories. These anti-imperialists felt it was unconstitutional to own colonies and a violation of the spirit of the Declaration of Independence to govern a foreign territory without the consent of its inhabitants. Outstanding opponents included such varied individuals as Andrew Carnegie, Samuel Gompers, William James, Mark Twain, and Jane Addams.

Philippines

1899–1901. Filipino nationalists under Emilio Aguinaldo resisted American occupation with guerrilla warfare.

1901. William Howard Taft became the first civilian governor.

1946. The Philippines became an independent Republic.

Puerto Rico

1901, Foraker Act. Established a civil government for Puerto Rico and placed tariff duties on Puerto Rican products brought into the United States.

1917. Puerto Rico received United States citizenship.

1952. Puerto Rico became an independent commonwealth. It is associated with the United States and can send nonvoting delegates to Congress, but the island is fully self-governing internally.

Cuba

General Leonard Wood (1860–1927). Military governor of Cuba from 1899 to 1902. He and the American occupation troops did a great deal to modernize sugar production, improve sanitary conditions, establish schools, and restore orderly administration.

1901, Platt Amendment. An amendment which the United States forced the Cubans to add to their constitution. It authorized American intervention when necessary to preserve Cuban independence and to maintain a Cuban government "adequate for the protection of life, property, and individual liberty." In addition Cuba could not make treaties which might compromise its independence. This provision referred in part to large loans which the Cuban government might not be able to repay and which would lead to foreign troops being sent in to demand payment. Finally, Cuba was to grant naval bases on its soil to the United States, and in 1903 the United States worked out an agreement for Guantanamo Bay.

1902. Cuba became an independent republic.

Expansionism Without Colonies

Dominican Republic. This Caribbean country had defaulted on debts to European bankers, and in 1903 these nations considered sending troops to force repayment. President Theodore Roosevelt said that if any country were going to take over the customs house, the only major source of revenue, the United States would, for European interference in this hemisphere was not allowed under the Monroe Doctrine.

1904, *Roosevelt Corollary* to the Monroe Doctrine. An expression of Roosevelt's Latin American policy as presented in a message to Congress in December 1904. He stated that "chronic wrongdoing" in Latin America might force the United States to step in and act as "an international police force." The immediate effect of the policy was to put the Dominican republic's finances in order, but in the long run it caused much resentment in Latin America.

China. This formerly powerful Asian empire had suffered political and economic upheavals, and Japan and European nations had moved in to carve out "spheres of influence," that is, areas in which they controlled local political leaders and obtained special trading privileges.

1899–1900, "Open Door" notes. Diplomatic dispatches sent by Secretary of State John Hay to Japan and to European powers asking them to guarantee that China could open its trading doors equally to all powers and that safeguards would be taken to prevent China's political takeover by any one power. The nations' replies were noncommittal, but since they had not openly refused, Hay announced that the powers had accepted the Open Door policy. In reality nothing had been accomplished, but the Open Door marked a great departure from traditional American isolation.

Japan. A rapidly industrializing nation with expansionist designs in the Far East and in the Pacific.

1905, Treaty of Portsmouth, New Hampshire. An agreement which ended the Russo-Japanese War.

1907, "Gentlemen's Agreement." Roosevelt persuaded the San Francisco school board to stop segregating oriental children, an action which the Japanese had protested. In exchange, Japan agreed not to issue passports to laborers seeking to come to America.

Panama. A province of Colombia which revolted in 1903, became an independent republic, and granted the United States a favorable treaty to build a canal across the isthmus.

1850, Clayton-Bulwer Treaty. An agreement between the United States and Great Britain that neither nation would "obtain or maintain for itself any exclusive control" over an interoceanic canal. This agreement was cancelled by the Hay-Pauncefote Treaty (1901) which transferred this right to the United States.

1903, Hay-Herrán Treaty. An agreement between the United States and Colombia which the Colombian senate refused to ratify. It would have given the United States a 99-year lease on a 6-mile wide zone in Panama through which to build a canal.

1903, Hay–Bunau-Varilla Treaty. A treaty between the United States and the newly independent Republic of Panama which granted the United States a 10-mile wide zone in perpetuity, that is, forever. The United States paid $10 million to Panama plus an annual rental of $250,000, a figure which has been greatly increased over the years. Within the Canal Zone the United States could act as if it were "the sovereign of the territory."

1914. Panama Canal was opened to ships.

1921. The United States paid Colombia $25 million for her loss of Panama, and in exchange, Colombia recognized the independence of the Republic of Panama.

American Policy

Imperialism. A policy of occupying and governing foreign lands which the United States followed between 1898 and 1903. The colonies acquired during these years were Hawaii, the Philippines, Guam, and Puerto Rico, all in 1898; Samoa, 1899; and the Guantanamo base and the Canal Zone, in 1903.

"Non-colonial imperial expansion." Term used by historian William Appleman Williams to describe America's policy of profitable economic penetration of underdeveloped areas without the trouble of owning and controlling them. Many felt that the "American way of life" would also be duplicated in these countries. Examples of this policy were Hay's Open Door notes (1899–1900) concerning China, the Roosevelt Corollary (1904) involving the Dominican Republic, and dollar diplomacy.

Dollar diplomacy. The term used by President William Howard Taft (1903–1913) to describe "non-colonial imperial expansion." His theory was that American economic penetration by private investors would bring stability to underdeveloped areas and power and profit to the United States without committing American troops or spending public funds. The theory did not always work, but examples of dollar diplomacy could be seen in Manchuria, Nicaragua, and Mexico.

Isolationism. Notwithstanding its expansionist policies in some areas, the United States remained psychologically isolationist, particularly toward Europe.

OTHER TERMS TO IDENTIFY

1871, Treaty of Washington. An agreement between the United States and Great Britain whereby the two nations agreed to arbitrate the so-called *Alabama* claims. These claims involved the United States' demands that Britain pay for the loss of some 100,000 tons of Union shipping sunk by Confederate cruisers that had been built in British shipyards during the Civil War. The *Alabama* was one of these ships. In 1872 the judges awarded the United States $15.5 million for the ships and cargoes that had been destroyed.

Archduke Maximilian (1832–1867). The younger brother of the Austrian emperor, who became Emperor of Mexico (1864–1867) with the support of Napoleon III and French troops. In 1866 Secretary of State William Seward officially protested the French intervention, and 50,000 American troops moved to the Rio Grande River. The following year the French troops were withdrawn, and Maximilian was shot by order of the Mexican nationalist, Benito Juarez.

1867, Purchase of Alaska. The Russian colony of Alaska was purchased by the United States at the instigation of Secretary of State Seward for $7.2 million.

1870, Annexation treaty with the Dominican Republic. The Dominicans desired to be annexed to the United States rather than be overrun once again by their neighbor, Haiti. President Grant worked out a treaty, but it was rejected by the United States Senate. This action reflected the antiexpansionist tendencies still in existence at this time.

Henry Cabot Lodge (1850–1924). Republican congressman from Massachusetts from 1886 until 1893, and then senator from 1893 to 1924, where he became chairman of the Senate Foreign Relations Committee. While still a member of the House, he was on the Naval Affairs Committee and advocated expanding and modernizing the fleet.

1823, Monroe Doctrine. Several passages in President Monroe's annual message which stated that North and South America were no longer open to colonization and that any attempt of European nations to intervene in this hemisphere would be considered a threat to the United States' security. This statement was not accepted as international law, but was repeatedly brought up, as in the 1895 Venezuela-British Guiana border dispute and in the 1904 Dominican Republic's customs collection problem.

Rough Riders. A volunteer regiment in the Spanish-American War under Colonel Leonard Wood and Lieutenant Colonel Theodore Roosevelt. The First Regiment of United States Cavalry Volunteers, including cowboys, Indians, and adventurous college students, was recruited by Roosevelt, trained in San Antonio, Texas, and made its famous charge up San Juan Hill on foot because their horses had been abandoned in Florida.

"Insular cases." A series of Supreme Court decisions between 1901 and 1922 which defined the constitutional status of the colonies. The general trend was that the Constitution did not follow the flag and that Congress could govern the areas as it pleased.

Philippe Bunau-Varilla (1859–1940). A French engineer who had heavy investments in the New Panama Canal Company and helped sway the United States toward a Panama route for a canal rather than one through Nicaragua. When Panama won its independence from Colombia, he was appointed minister to Washington and negotiated the 1903 Hay–Bunau-Varilla Treaty for the Canal Zone.

Elihu Root (1845–1937). A corporation lawyer who was secretary of war from 1899 to 1904 and secretary of state from 1905 to 1909.

GLOSSARY

Achilles' heel. In Greek mythology, Achilles was the foremost hero of the Trojan War as described by Homer in the *Iliad*. According to legend, his mother bathed him in the river Styx to make him immortal, and the only place where he remained vulnerable was the heel where she held him. Theodore Roosevelt commented that the Philippines were "our heel of Achilles," indefensible in the case of a Japanese attack.

archipelago. A large group of islands. After the Spanish-American War, the expansionists were eager to annex the entire archipelago of the Philippine Islands.

arson. The crime of deliberately burning the building or property of another. Tales of rape, arson, and murder by United States troops in the Philippines provided ammunition for the anti-imperialists.

Boxer Rebellion. A nationalist uprising in China in 1900 directed against the Empress and the foreign nations that had established spheres of influence. Great Britain, Russia, Germany, France, Japan, and the United States sent in 5,000 troops to lift the siege of the legations in Peking.

chargé d'affaires. A diplomatic representative of the lowest rank. Tomás Herrán was the Colombian chargé in Washington in 1903.

Diplomatic ranks in order of their importance are:

    ambassador
    envoy extraordinary and minister plenipotentiary
    minister
    chargé d'affaires

coup. A brilliantly executed maneuver. It is also short for coup d'état, a French term meaning an overthrow of a government. In 1893 Americans in Hawaii helped stage a coup to overthrow Queen Liliuokalani.

dago. A derogatory slang word generally used to refer to Italians, Spaniards, or Portuguese. It was also used to refer to Spanish-Americans. During the Spanish-American War, some Americans referred to the Cuban insurgents as "thieving dagoes," and after the Panamanian revolt, Roosevelt referred to the Colombians as "dagoes."

ensign. A national flag displayed on ships or aircraft or the flag of a military unit. After the war in Cuba, order and prosperity did not automatically appear when the red and gold ensigns of Spain were hauled down from the flagstaffs of Havana and Santiago.

hallmark. An obvious indication of the quality or character of something. For example, whether one sees isolation or expansion as the hallmark, or outstanding characteristic, of American foreign policy after 1865 depends upon what part of the world one views. Originally, a hallmark was a mark used in England to stamp gold and silver articles that met established standards of purity. The term was taken from Goldsmith's Hall in London, where gold and silver articles were appraised and stamped.

heathen. One who did not believe in the God of Christianity, Judaism, or Islam, and therefore was viewed by converts of those religions as being uncivilized or unenlightened. American expansionists were influenced by British liberals who in the 1870s and 1880s began to stress a "duty" to spread Christianity among the heathen.

Nobel prize. Any of the prizes awarded annually by the Nobel Foundation for outstanding achievements in the fields of medicine, chemistry, physics, and literature and for the promotion of world peace. Money for the prizes was provided for in the will of Alfred Bernhard Nobel (1833–1896), a Swedish chemist and inventor. Theodore Roosevelt received the Nobel Peace Prize for arbitrating the Russo-Japanese war in 1905.

peonage. A system in which debtors are bound in servitude to their creditors until the debts are paid. In this manner many unskilled farm workers in Latin America became virtual slaves of the big landowners. After Cuban independence many peasants continued to live in a state of peonage on great sugar plantations.

revenue cutter. A boat used by government officials to patrol the coastlines and make sure that products are not brought into the country illegally, that is, without paying the import duties.

vassal. A person in the Middle Ages who held land from a feudal lord and received protection from him in exchange for loyalty and allegiance. A vassal state is similar except that a country becomes subordinate to or dependent on another country. Anti-imperialists did not want to take over vassal states such as the Philippines.

Yanqui. The Spanish word for Yankee, which was used in Latin America to refer to all United States citizens, regardless of the part of the country they were from. Anti-*Yanqui* feeling was often high.

WORDS TO KNOW

Define the following, using the dictionary if necessary.

ambivalent	hegemony
asperity	intrepid
endemic	oligarchic
exacerbated	salubrious
fiat	supercilious

SAMPLE QUESTIONS

Multiple Choice

1. The naval captain who wrote that the United States should have bases in the Caribbean, cut a canal across Central America, and annex Hawaii was:
   a. George Dewey.
   b. William T. Sampson.
   c. Stephen B. Luce.
   d. Alfred Thayer Mahan.
2. The "insular cases" determined that:
   a. the United States could lawfully annex islands such as Puerto Rico.
   b. the United States had the sole right to build a transisthmian canal.
   c. the Constitution does not follow the flag.
   d. colonials had all rights granted to Americans.
3. The statement that "chronic wrongdoing" might necessitate the United States acting as an "international police force" was expressed in the:
   a. Open Door notes.
   b. Roosevelt Corollary.
   c. Teller Amendment.
   d. Treaty of Washington.
4. The Open Door policy stated that:
   a. all nations were to have equal trading opportunities with China.
   b. Japan should open her ports to the rest of the world.
   c. each nation should have its "sphere of influence" in China.
   d. each nation should receive indemnities for life and property lost in the Boxer Rebellion.
5. President Taft's policy of encouraging American entrepreneurs to invest in underdeveloped countries rather than committing public funds was known as:
   a. dollar diplomacy.
   b. Open Door policy.

    c. Colonial imperialism.

    d. "Gentlemen's Agreement."

Matching

Match the appropriate country with the numbered entries. Some countries may be named more than once.

1. ____Clayton-Bulwer Treaty	a. China
2. ____Platt Amendment	b. Panama
3. ____Hay–Bunau-Varilla Treaty	c. Japan
4. ____Foraker Act	d. Dominican Republic
5. ____Open Door notes	e. Great Britain
6. ____*Alabama* claims	f. Cuba
7. ____Teller Amendment	g. Puerto Rico
8. ____Gentlemen's Agreement	
9. ____*Maine* explosion	
10. ____Roosevelt Corollary	

ANSWERS

Multiple Choice: d, c, b, a. Matching: e, f, b, g, a, e, f, c, f, d.

23

The Progressive Era

CHRONOLOGY

1905   Niagara Falls meeting
1906   Pure Food and Drug Act
1909   NAACP founded
1910   Ballinger-Pinchot controversy
1912   Progressive party in 1912 election
1913   Seventeenth Amendment—direct election of senators
1914   Clayton Antitrust Act
1920   Nineteenth Amendment—women's suffrage

CHAPTER CHECKLIST

Expressions of Progressivism

Progressivism. A reform movement most active from around 1898–1914. Progressives were not a unified group but individuals interested in improving their society, especially in three areas. One was to fight corruption and inefficiency in government; a second was to regulate and control big business; and a third, to obtain social-welfare legislation to improve the conditions of the urban poor.

Muckraker. An individual, usually a journalist, who wrote exposes on corrupt situations with the hope of bringing about reform. The term was first coined by Theodore Roosevelt, who compared these journalists to "the Man with the Muck-Rake" in John Bunyan's *Pilgrim's Progress* (1678). Famous muckrakers included Ida Tarbell, who wrote about Standard Oil, and Lincoln Steffens, who exposed urban political machines. *McClure's* was one famous magazine which carried these articles.

"Ashcan" artists. Artists who were sympathetic with social reform and tried to develop a distinctively American style which would probe the world they lived in. Robert Henri, John Sloan, and George Luks were "ashcan" artists.

Reforming the Political System

City Level

Abe Ruef. A clever lawyer who became the political boss of San Francisco in the early 1900s and whose activities were typical of corruption in the city government. Ruef's machine was finally broken, and he was jailed.

City-manager system. A form of municipal government designed to eliminate corruption and political machines. The professional manager was appointed by the city commission to administer city affairs on a nonpartisan basis.

State level

Robert La Follette (1855–1925). An outstanding politician who made Wisconsin the model for state progressivism. His political career was long: Republican congressman (1885–1891), governor (1901–1906), and senator (1906–1925). As governor, La Follette overhauled the political structure of the state, introducing the direct primary for nominating party candidates and laws limiting lobbying activities, establishing a legislative reference library, and bringing in scholars and specialists as governmental advisers. Other states copied the "Wisconsin Idea," that is, progressive measures at the state level.

National level

Women's suffrage. The struggle for women's right to vote culminated in the Nineteenth Amendment to the Constitution which went into effect in 1920. The movement was led by the National American Women's Suffrage Association, which at first had concentrated on a state-by-state approach to suffrage, and by the Congressional Union, which wanted change at the national level.

Changes in Congress. The Seventeenth Amendment (1913) required senators to be elected by the people rather than by the state legislatures. The House of Representatives was reformed by limiting the power of the speaker, Joseph Cannon, who had continued the tyrannies of "Czar" Thomas Reed, speaker in the 1890s.

Social and Economic Reform

City "gas and water socialism." Public utility companies were taken over and operated as departments of the municipal government. By 1915 nearly two-thirds of all city waterworks were publicly owned.

Children. The National Child Labor Committee, started in 1904, successfully lobbied for state laws banning the employment of young children and limiting the working hours of older children to eight or ten per day.

Hammer v. *Dagenhart* (1918). A Supreme Court decision which declared a 1916 federal child labor law unconstitutional.

Women. By 1917 nearly all states had placed limitations on the hours of women employed in industry, and ten states had set minimum wage standards for women.

Muller v. *Oregon* (1908). The Supreme Court upheld an Oregon law limiting women laundry workers to ten hours a day. The attorney who presented the case for Oregon was Louis Brandeis, who was later appointed to the Supreme Court by Woodrow Wilson. The case was particularly significant because of the use of the *Brandeis brief* technique, that is, Brandeis used physiological, sociological, and economic data as well as legal evidence to argue his case.

Adkins v. *Children's Hospital* (1923). A Supreme Court decision which declared a ten-hour law for women workers in the District of Columbia unconstitutional. Note that Washington, D.C.'s laws were passed by Congress, not by a state legislature, whose powers in this area had already been recognized.

On-the-job accidents. By 1916 nearly three-quarters of the states had adopted accident insurance systems. Stricter municipal building codes and state factory inspection acts were also passed to protect the worker.

THEODORE ROOSEVELT (1858–1919), 26th President

Born in New York and graduated from Harvard.
Served as a New York State assemblyman and as president of the New York City Board of Police Commissioners.
Assistant secretary of the navy (1897–1898), and an officer of the Rough Riders in the Spanish-American War.
Republican governor of New York (1899–1901).
Vice-president under McKinley (1901).
President after McKinley's assassination and then reelected for a full term (1901–1909).
Unsuccessful Progressive party candidate for the presidency in 1912.

Roosevelt's Trustbusting

Northern Securities Company case. In 1902 the Justice Department sued this railroad holding company for violating the Sherman Antitrust Act. A holding company is one which exists solely to own the stocks or securities of other companies. The Northern Securities Company had been set up in 1901 to control the Great Northern; the Northern Pacific; and the Chicago, Burlington, and Quincy railroads. In 1904 the Court ordered the Northern Securities Company to dissolve, and shortly thereafter the government filed suits against other monopolies.

"Gentlemen's agreement." Negotiated settlement between a corporation and President Roosevelt in which the corporation privately agreed to correct any malpractices in exchange for the government not filing an antitrust suit against it. Such informal arrangements were made with U.S. Steel in 1905 and with International Harvester in 1907, revealing that Roosevelt was not always opposed to trusts and that those which conformed to his somewhat subjective standards could remain as they were.

Roosevelt's Labor Policies

1902, Anthracite coal strike. A strike of the United Mine Workers, led by John Mitchell, for higher wages, an eight-hour day, and recognition of their union, that is, that the mine owners would sit down and bargain with them as equals. The mine owners refused to negotiate and shut down their mines, which not only starved the workers but threatened a coal shortage. President Roosevelt, who sympathized with the miners, called a conference of both sides in Washington, and when the owners refused to bargain, he threatened to send in federal troops to seize and operate the mines. Under this threat, the owners agreed to submit the dispute to a presidentially appointed commission which, in March 1903, granted the miners a 10 percent wage increase and a nine-hour day. The owners, however, were not required to recognize the United Mine Workers.

"Square deal." A term sometimes used to refer to Roosevelt's labor policy, that he wanted a "square deal" for labor. It was also used to refer to his general platform in the 1904 election.

Regulating Big Business

1903, Department of Commerce and Labor created. It included a Bureau of Corporations with authority to investigate industrial mergers. The department was divided into two Cabinet-level posts in 1913.

1903, Elkins Act. A measure designed to strengthen the Interstate Commerce Commission by making it illegal for a business to receive rebates rather than just punishing the railroads granting them. It also forbade railroads to deviate from their published rates. The act was not successful because federal courts continued to favor the railroads in most cases.

1906, Hepburn Act. An act which strengthened the Interstate Commerce Commission by affirming its right to regulate not only railroads, but also sleeping car companies, owners of oil pipelines, and other firms engaged in transportation. It further gave the commission the power to inspect the financial records of railroads and to fix rates.

1906, Meat inspection. An act setting meat packing standards was passed after the publication of Upton Sinclair's *The Jungle,* a novel exposing the filthy conditions in the Chicago slaughterhouses.

1906, Pure Food and Drug Act. An act forbidding the manufacture and sale of dishonestly labeled products.

Conservation

1902, Newlands Act. A measure stating that money from the sale of public land in the West would be used for federal irrigation projects.

1908, National Conservation Conference. A meeting in Washington attended by 44 governors and 500 other persons to discuss conservation. As a result, most states created their own conservation commissions.

WILLIAM HOWARD TAFT (1857–1930), 27th President

Born in Ohio and educated at Yale and at the Cincinnati Law School.
Served as an Ohio judge, as solicitor general of the United States, and as a federal circuit court judge.
Governor of the Philippines (1901–1904).
Secretary of war (1904–1908).
President (1909–1913).
Chief justice of the Supreme Court (1921–1930).

Taft's Presidency

Progressive measures. Taft vigorously enforced the Sherman Antitrust Act, added to the national forest reserves, supported an eight-hour day for all persons engaged in work on government contracts, and promoted mine-safety legislation.

1910, Mann-Elkins Act. Strengthened the Interstate Commerce Commission by empowering it to suspend rate increases without waiting for a shipper to complain and by establishing a Commerce Court to speed the settlement of railroad rate litigation.

1909, Payne-Aldrich Tariff. A controversial tariff backed by Taft. The original bill in the House of Representatives made substantial rate reductions and placed several items on the free list. But the Senate Finance Committee, chaired by Nelson Aldrich of Rhode Island, made numerous amendments, most of which raised rates and took items off the free list. "Insurgent," or rebel, Republican senators fought these increases, but the measure passed and Taft called it "the best bill that the Republican party ever passed." The debate marked the beginning of the Republican split of 1912.

1910, Ballinger-Pinchot controversy. Chief Forester Gifford Pinchot accused Secretary of the Interior Richard Ballinger of not adequately protecting natural resources from private exploitation. President Taft decided that the charges were unjust and dismissed Pinchot, thereby angering the conservationists. The affair was further complicated by the fact that Pinchot was a personal friend of Roosevelt who went to him with complaints from party progressives asking him to resume leadership.

Election of 1912

Republican: William Howard Taft. Taft controlled the party machinery and was able to get the nomination on the first ballot. He had the support of the Old Guard, or conservative, Republicans.

Progressive: Theodore Roosevelt. The Republican party split, and the progressive faction set up a new party. The organization was sometimes called the Bull Moose party, after a statement by Roosevelt that he felt "as strong as a bull moose."

New Nationalism. The name given to Roosevelt's progressive platform. He first used the phrase in a 1910 speech in Osawatomie, Kansas, attacking the Supreme Court's view toward social legislation. Concerning big business, Roosevelt proclaimed that trusts were not bad as long as they were subject to federal regulation.

Democrat: Woodrow Wilson. The Democratic convention finally nominated Wilson, the progressive governor of New Jersey, on the 46th ballot.

New Freedom. The name given to Wilson's platform. Wilson felt the government could best serve social justice by getting rid of all special privileges. Rather than following Roosevelt's plan of letting monopolies exist and having the government regulate them, Wilson insisted that free competition be restored. Instead of regulating monopoly, the government should regulate competition.

The Democrat, Woodrow Wilson, won the election. Note the map entitled "The Election of 1912" on p. 585.

WOODROW WILSON (1856–1924), 28th President

Born in Virginia. Took degress from Princeton, the University of Virginia Law School, and Johns Hopkins.

Taught political science at various colleges and then became president of Princeton (1902–1910).

Democratic governor of New Jersey (1911–1913).

President (1913–1921).

Wilson's New Freedom

1913, Underwood Tariff. The first significant reduction in import duties since 1860. Items which could be produced more cheaply in the United

States than abroad, such as food, wool, iron and steel, shoes, and agricultural machinery, were placed on the free list, and the rates on other products were substantially cut. To make up for the expected loss of revenue, a graduated tax on personal incomes was included in the act. The income tax had been made constitutional by the Sixteenth Amendment.

1913, Federal Reserve Act. An act which set up a national banking system for the United States.

Federal Reserve Bank in each of 12 banking districts. Each region has a central headquarters, or Federal Reserve Bank, which serves as a bank for bankers in that area. To learn some of these headquarters, look on the front of a piece of paper money for a letter of the alphabet, A through L, and then note the city under it. For example K means that the money was issued in Dallas, Texas.

Federal Reserve Board. The coordinating board in Washington made up of the secretary of the treasury, the comptroller of the currency, and six financial experts appointed by the president.

1914, Federal Trade Commission. A presidentially appointed board with the power to investigate interstate corporations and to issue "cease and desist" orders against "unfair" trade practices. It was designed to protect the public against the trusts.

1914, Clayton Antitrust Act. An act which made certain business practices illegal, such as "tying" agreements which forbade retailers from handling competitors' products. It also forbade interlocking directorates as a means of controlling competing companies, that is, some members of one board of directors also sitting on the board of other companies so as to control their activities in a complimentary rather than in a competing fashion. Furthermore, the officers of corporations could be held individually responsible when their companies violated the antitrust laws. The Clayton Act also exempted labor unions and farmers' organizations from antitrust laws.

Progressivism and the Race Issue

William E. B. Du Bois (1868–1963). The well-educated leader of militant blacks. He rejected Booker T. Washington's acceptance of second-class citizenship and was outraged by white treatment of blacks. Du Bois felt that blacks should be proud of their origins and culture and should try to preserve their identity. He helped organize the Niagara Movement and became a national officer in the National Association for the Advancement of Colored People and editor of its journal, *The Crisis.*

1905, Niagara Falls meeting. A gathering of Du Bois and a few like-minded blacks in Niagara Falls, New York. They issued a list of demands: the unrestricted right to vote, an end to all segregation, equal economic opportunity, the right to higher education, equal justice in the courts, and an end to discrimination in trade unions. The Niagara Movement did not attract much black support, but did reach some liberal whites.

1909, National Association for the Advancement of Colored People. An organization founded by a group of liberals, including Oswald Garrison Villard, Jane Addams, John Dewey, and William Dean Howells, to wipe out racial discrimination.

OTHER TERMS TO IDENTIFY

"Municipal socialism." Public ownership of streetcars, waterworks, and other local utilities.

Socialist party. A political party organized in 1901 and led by Eugene Debs until his death in 1926. Socialists advocated government rather than private ownership of the means of production and distribution. They gained considerable strength during the progressive era, although progressives would have little to do with them.

1913, Armory Show. An art exhibit sponsored by the Association of American Painters and Sculptors and held in New York's 69th Regiment Armory. The works of the American "ashcan" artists were virtually ignored while the European postimpressionist paintings stole the show.

Samuel "Golden Rule" Jones (1846–1904). Progressive mayor of Toledo, Ohio, first as a Republican then as an independent, from 1897 to 1904. During his terms he established a minimum wage for city employees, built playgrounds and golf courses, and moderated Toledo's harsh penal code.

Carrie Chapman Catt (1859–1947). A suffragist who became president of the National American Women's Suffrage Association in 1900 and who was a leader of the campaign for a constitutional amendment to give women the vote. After ratification of the Nineteenth Amendment (1920), she organized the League of Women Voters.

National Progressive Republican League. The liberal faction of the Republican party, organized in January 1911, which backed Robert La Follette as the Republican candidate for the 1912 race and then switched to Theodore Roosevelt.

Herbert Croly (1869–1930). Author and editor whose book, *The Promise of American Life* (1909), provided the title and many ideas of Roosevelt's "new nationalism." Croly advocated Hamiltonian means to achieve Jeffersonian ends, that is, the national government should take a more active role in regulating the economy in order to preserve the individual freedoms valued by Jefferson.

Carter G. Woodson. A black leader who in 1915 founded the Association for the Study of Negro Life and History and in 1916 began editing the scholarly *Journal of Negro History*.

GLOSSARY

accommodation. Booker T. Washington's policy of urging blacks to accept segregation. He felt that blacks would eventually achieve social equality if, for the present, they would concentrate on learning a trade and making economic gains rather than on obtaining political power or higher education.

bull. An official document issued by the Pope and sealed with a *bulla,* which is a round seal affixed to the papal bull. In 1900 Roosevelt stated that much of the antitrust legislation was "not one whit more intelligent than the medieval bull against the comet."

caucus. A meeting of the members of a political party to decide questions of policy and to select candidates for office. After 1910, appointments to committees in the House of Representatives were determined by the whole membership, acting through party caucuses, rather than by the speaker of the House.

cubism. A school of painting and sculpture developed in the early 20th century which represented natural forms and images using geometric patterns. The term is from a remark by Henri Matisse concerning the "small cubes" which predominated in a painting by Georges Braque. A cubist painting, Marcel Duchamp's *Nude Descending a Staircase,* became the focal point of the 1913 Armory Show in New York.

direct primary. An election by the registered voters of a party for the purpose of nominating candidates. The winners of the primary then run against the other parties' candidates in the regular election. The direct primary system of nominating candidates, rather than the party caucus system, was introduced in the states as a progressive reform, designed to bring the government closer to the people.

extralegal. Outside of or beyond the law. The committee appointed by Roosevelt to arbitrate the 1902 coal strike was extralegal, for there was no law providing for such a measure.

grassroots campaign. A political campaign which concentrates on an area or people somewhat isolated from a major political center. It is an appeal to the common man. Robert La Follette won elections by vigorous grassroots campaigning.

Huguenot. A French Protestant, that is, non-Roman Catholic Christian, of the 16th and 17th centuries. The father of W. E. B. Du Bois was a restless wanderer of black and French Huguenot stock.

insurgent. One who revolts against authority, especially a member of a political party who rebels against its leadership. The liberal progressives who rebelled against the conservative Republican leaders were called insurgents.

postal savings system. A government savings bank operated through local post offices from 1910 to 1966. It received savings deposits from $5 to $2,500 from any person ten years of age or older, and paid 2 percent interest. It was designed to provide easy and safe banking for small accounts.

retainer. A fee paid to a lawyer or other professional to regularly engage the person's services. The lawyer Abe Ruef, city boss of San Francisco, collected $1,000 a month from the local gas company as a "retainer," which in actuality was more like a payoff.

rider. A clause added to a legislative bill which usually has little relevance to the main bill. Riders are frequently added to essential appropriation, or money, bills, which most congressmen feel must be passed quickly and therefore the additions will be tolerated.

Rules Committee. A committee of the House of Representatives which determines the priority of bills to be brought to a vote. The committee grants special rules for handling a bill which may permit or forbid amendments, sets the length of debate, and otherwise speeds or slows up the bill. In 1910 the insurgents stripped Speaker of the House Joseph Cannon of his control over the House Rules Committee, through which he had virtually been able to control which bills became law.

Sirens. In Greek mythology, the Sirens were sea nymphs who inhabited an island surrounded by dangerous rocks. They sang so enchantingly that all who heard drew near and were shipwrecked. In the *Odyssey,* a Greek epic poem, Odysseus escaped the Sirens by having himself tied to a mast and by stopping the ears of his sailors.

solicitor general. The attorney who presents the federal government's cases before the Supreme Court.

Victorian. Pertaining to the period of Queen Victoria, ruler of the British Empire from 1837 to 1901. One characteristic of the era was an emphasis on being morally straitlaced, at least on the surface. Topics pertaining to sex were taboo in "polite society." Feminist leaders in the late 19th century were somewhat handicapped by the Victorian idealization of female "purity."

WORDS TO KNOW

Define the following, using the dictionary if necessary.

antipathetic	monolithic
blandishment	preternatural
continence	rapaciousness
implacable	spate

SAMPLE QUESTIONS

Multiple Choice

1. The following were all characteristics of the progressive movement *except:*
   a. a desire to regulate big business.
   b. a commitment to black equality.
   c. a desire to make government responsive to the people.
   d. concern for the welfare of the urban poor.
2. Seventeenth Amendment:
   a. popular election of United States senators.
   b. the right of the federal government to levy a personal income tax.
   c. prohibition of manufacture and sale of alcoholic beverages.
   d. right of women to vote.
3. Meat inspection legislation was accelerated by:
   a. the crusades of Abe Ruef.
   b. Taft's concern for the public health.
   c. Upton Sinclair's *The Jungle.*
   d. Lincoln Steffens' muckracking articles.
4. In 1909 a group of progressives started an organization whose aim was to abolish segregation and obtain civil rights for blacks. The organization was called:
   a. WCTU.
   b. Tuskegee movement.
   c. NAACP.
   d. ACLU.
5. The New Freedom favored:
   a. the welfare state.
   b. the restoration of competition.
   c. unlimited laissez faire.
   d. government ownership of railroads.

True-False

1. The "Wisconsin Idea" was the progressive program of Robert La Follette.
2. In *Muller* v. *Oregon* (1908) the Supreme Court upheld an Oregon law limiting women laundry workers to ten hours a day.
3. President Roosevelt adopted a "hands off" policy toward the 1902 anthracite coal strike.
4. New Nationalism favored a laissez faire policy.
5. At the Niagara Falls meeting, W. E. B. Du Bois rejected the Booker T. Washington approach to race problems.

Multiple Choice: b, a, c, c, b. True-False: T, T, F, F, T.
ANSWERS

Portfolio Five
Women's Lot

PORTFOLIO CHECKLIST

Women's Occupations in the Late 19th Century

Homemaker. Most women married, reared children, kept house, and if financially possible, did not work outside the home. By the late 1880s, new household appliances were beginning to ease the domestic routine.

Domestic worker. About one-third of working women were servants in other people's homes, in hotels, laundries, and similar service industries.

Factory worker. A good percentage of women worked in textile and garment-making plants, making low wages and tolerating deplorable working conditions. But few joined trade unions before the early 1900s, when the International Ladies Garment Workers' Union became the largest representative of women workers. In 1910 only 5 percent of women factory workers belonged to unions.

Farm laborer. Women worked in all kinds of farm labor positions. In the South, cotton picking was a major occupation, particularly for blacks.

Office worker. Secretaries, typists, stenographers, and clerks increased in number after 1900. The advent of the typewriter, still a novelty in the 1880s, opened new opportunities for women.

Painter. Mary Cassatt, the impressionist painter, frequently portrayed in her works the special relationship between women and their children. Cassatt chose to follow a profession rather than marry.

Actress. A few stars, such as Maude Adams, had glamorous careers and substantial incomes. Adams, after 50 years in the theater, became a teacher of dramatics at a women's college in Missouri.

Teacher. Most women college graduates went into teaching. By 1890 two-thirds of American schoolteachers were women.

Nurse. The first American schools of nursing opened in the 1870s, preparing nurses to work in slums and schools as well as in hospitals. In 1893

Lillian Wald organized a visiting-nurse service in New York City, after discovering that 90 percent of the ill in cities were confined to home, not in hospitals.

Prostitute. Girls usually became prostitutes around the age of 16, some voluntarily and some procured by devious means. In 1910 Congress passed the White Slave Traffic Act, which put heavy penalties on the transport of women into the country or between states for immoral purposes.

Social worker. Jane Addams' Hull House in Chicago and Lillian Wald's Henry Street Settlement in New York City provided social services in slum neighborhoods. Through their efforts and others, another profession—social work—emerged as a career for educated women. Most of the openings, however, were volunteer jobs.

OTHER TERMS TO IDENTIFY

M. Carey Thomas (1857–1935). An educator who helped organized Bryn Mawr college for women in Pennsylvania in 1884 and became its president from 1894 to 1922. She was also active in the women's suffrage movement which culminated in the Nineteenth Amendment (1920).

Triangle fire. In 1911 a fire ravaged the Triangle Shirtwaist Company in New York City, killing over 140 garment workers. A public protest meeting pointed out that the building was a firetrap and that the company felt little responsibility for its employees.

Rose Schneiderman (1884–1972). A Polish immigrant who became a nationally known women's trade union organizer. As an executive of the Women's Trade Union League, it was her job to support unions that had women members.

GLOSSARY

foundry. A factory in which metals were melted and poured into molds. According to one labor leader, women workers sometimes stripped to the waist because of the heat.

piecework. Work paid for according to the number of products turned out rather than the number of hours worked. Piecework for garment manufacturers was often done by women and children working in their slum apartments.

shirtwaist. A woman's tailored blouse or dress with details copied from men's shirts.

waiver. A document which states the intentional giving up of a right or claim. Most employers made parents sign waivers in the event of a child's injury on the job.

WORDS TO KNOW

Define the following, using the dictionary if necessary.

brothel	potash
chattel	ticker tape
militate	viselike

24

Woodrow Wilson and the Great War

CHRONOLOGY

1914 Veracruz crisis in Mexico
1914 Assassination of archduke in Austria-Hungary
1915 Sinking of the *Lusitania*
1916 Pershing expedition in Mexico
1917 Zimmermann telegram
1918 Wilson's "Fourteen Points" speech
1919 Treaty of Versailles

CHAPTER CHECKLIST

Wilson's Diplomacy

Missionary diplomacy. The idealistic diplomacy advocated by President Wilson. The United States' relations with other countries should be based "upon terms of equality and honor," and the monetary "interference" of Taft's dollar diplomacy should be avoided. Wilson followed this principle to a degree, but ignored it when it conflicted with what he considered the country's best interests.

Caribbean protectorates. Concern over the security of the Panama Canal made Wilson intolerant of unrest in the Caribbean area. When conflicts broke out he sent in marines to establish stable, although unpopular, governments in Nicaragua (1914), Haiti (1915), and the Dominican Republic (1916). The last troops were not withdrawn from these areas until the early 1930s as a result of Franklin Roosevelt's Good Neighbor policy.

MEXICO

1910, Mexican Revolution. An economic and political upheaval in which Porfirio Díaz, Mexico's dictator since 1876, was overthrown by the idealistic reformer, Francisco Madero. After a short period as president (1911–1913), Madero was ousted and ordered shot by a reactionary general, Victoriano Huerta. This action morally offended President Wilson, who refused diplomatic recognition of Huerta's government and brought pressure to bear upon his regime.

1914, Tampico incident. American sailors were arrested and promptly released in the Gulf of Mexico port of Tampico. But the Mexican government refused to deliver the formal apology demanded by the sailors' commander. This incident was later used as an excuse for troop intervention.

1914, Veracruz crisis. Wilson ordered American troops to occupy the port of Veracruz, so that a German ship could not unload munitions for Huerta's army. Instead of surrendering the port as Wilson had expected, the Mexicans resisted the takeover and suffered 400 casualties. This incident caused an outcry both in the United States and in Latin America.

1914, Niagara Falls conference. Three Latin American countries, Argentina, Brazil, and Chile, offered to mediate the dispute between the United States and Mexico, and representatives met on the Canadian side of the Falls. No agreement was reached, but the conference enabled the United States to avoid war.

1916–1917, Pershing expedition. A military advance into northern Mexico led by General John J. Pershing. The purpose of the expedition was to capture Pancho Villa, a Mexican revolutionary who had raided the town of Columbus, New Mexico, killing 19. Early in 1917, with the growing threat of the European war, Wilson recalled the troops, mission unaccomplished.

The War in Europe

June 28, 1914: Assassination of Archduke Franz Ferdinand. The heir to the Hapsburg throne of Austria-Hungary was shot in Sarajevo (in present-day Yugoslavia) by an assassin from the neighboring country of Serbia. When Austria-Hungary declared war on Serbia, the latter's ally, Russia, declared war on Austria-Hungary. Because of the network of alliances, all major European countries soon exchanged declarations of war.

Central Powers. The coalition of countries in World War I led by Germany and Austria-Hungary.

Allied Powers. The alliance in World War I led by Great Britain, France, and Russia, which was sometimes referred to as the Triple Entente. In 1917 the United States joined these countries as an "associated" power.

Proclamation of Neutrality. President Wilson proclaimed the United States officially neutral, and most Americans felt the war was of no concern to them. But a majority probably hoped for an allied victory.

Freedom of the Seas

Neutral rights. Under international law, neutrals could trade freely with any belligerent, that is, a country at war. However, the British fleet controlled the North Atlantic and tried to cut off shipping to Germany. Although Americans protested, they tolerated the blockade and traded more heavily with the Allies.

German U-boat. The German submarine, commonly called the U-boat, was a new weapon which could torpedo Allied ships without warning. In February 1915, the Germans announced a war zone around the British Isles, in which enemy ships would be sunk without warning and which neutrals entered at their own risk. Wilson protested and claimed he would hold the Germans to "strict accountability" for loss of American lives and property. Note the chart "U-boat Campaign, 1914–1918," on p. 644.

1915, Sinking of the *Lusitania*. The British liner *Lusitania* was sunk off the Irish coast by a German submarine. Nearly 1,200 persons, including 128 Americans, died—a fact which had great emotional impact in the United States. Wilson issued an ultimatum to the German government, but did not push it. After nearly a year, the Germans did issue an official apology and agree to indemnify the victims, that is, make monetary settlements with their survivors. Even Wilson's mild protests resulted in the resignation of Secretary of State William Jennings Bryan, who felt the United States was treating Germany and Allied violations of international law differently, and thus not being strictly neutral.

1916, *Sussex* pledge. After the French channel steamer *Sussex* was torpedoed and Americans on it were injured, Wilson sternly protested, and Germany promised to stop sinking merchantmen, that is, ships used in commerce, without warning. For nine months Germany kept this promise, and the United States had no complaints.

Election of 1916

Democrat: Woodrow Wilson. President Wilson had pushed many vote-winning progressive reform measures through Congress, including farm loans, workmen's compensation, and higher tariffs. But the chief issue was the American policy toward the European war, and the winning Democratic slogan became "He Kept Us Out of War."

Republican: Charles Evans Hughes. A former New York governor and Supreme Court justice, Hughes proved to be a poor political campaigner.

The Road to War

Colonel Edward House (1858–1938). A close friend of Wilson who made several trips to Europe attempting to mediate among the nations at war. House was later a delegate at the Paris Peace Conference at the end of the war. House was not in the military; "Colonel" was an honorary Texas title.

January 22, 1917: Wilson's "peace without victory" speech. An address before the Senate in which Wilson appealed to the people of the belligerent powers to stop fighting and work for world peace.

Resumption of submarine attacks. Germany announced that after February 1, 1917, submarines would be unleashed on all vessels headed for Allied ports. Germany was convinced that cutting off American supplies would bring the Allies to their knees. The United States might eventually enter the war as a result of renewed torpedoing, but not in time to be effective. When Germany carried out this threat on February 3 by torpedoing the U.S.S. *Housatonic,* Wilson broke diplomatic relations with Germany.

1917, Zimmermann telegram. A telegram from the German Secretary for Foreign Affairs Alfred Zimmermann to the German minister in Mexico, asking him to propose a military alliance with Mexico against the United States, promising Mexico the areas of Texas, New Mexico, and Arizona. The British intercepted the telegram and turned it over to the United States, where it further stirred anti-German feeling when it was released to the press on March 1.

Mobilization

Railroads. Secretary of the Treasury William McAdoo was appointed director-general of the railroads, with power to run the roads as a single system.

Conscription. After six weeks of debate, Congress finally voted to draft men between the ages of 21 and 30. It took nearly six more months before the draftees reached training camps.

Council of National Defense. A coordinating body for the manufacture of munitions and war goods which consisted of six Cabinet officers and a seven-man advisory commission. The Council lacked the authority to do the job properly.

War Industry Board. Created by the Council of National Defense, this board oversaw all aspects of industrial production and distribution. *Bernard Baruch* became its director in March 1918, and under him, the War Industry Board allocated scarce materials, standardized production, fixed prices, and coordinated American and Allied purchasing.

Food Administration. Herbert Hoover headed this program to stimulate food production and promote voluntary rationing.

Effects of the War Effort

Business. Antitrust laws were suspended, and manufacturers were allowed large profits. Close relations were also established between business and military leaders.

Labor. The war created full employment and greatly benefited labor. In April 1918, Wilson created a *National War Labor Board,* headed by former President Taft and Frank Walsh, to settle labor disputes and thus prevent strikes. A *War Labor Policies Board,* headed by Felix Frankfurter, laid down standard wages-and-hours patterns for war industries. Unionization and collective bargaining were encouraged by the administration.

War financing. There were five Victory and Liberty Loan drives in which people were encouraged to invest in war bonds. (See poster on p. 606.) The graduated income tax, an excess-profits tax, and an inheritance tax also contributed money to the government.

Information control. A Committee on Public Information headed by *George Creel* was created to sway public opinion behind the war effort.

1917, Espionage Act. Established fines and jail sentences for persons guilty of aiding the enemy or obstructing recruiting. It also authorized the postmaster general to ban treasonable or seditious material from the mails. The constitutionality of this law was upheld in the Supreme Court decision, *Schenck* v. *U.S.* (1919).

1918, Sedition Act. This act made it illegal to discourage the sale of war bonds or to criticize, orally or in writing, the government or the Constitution.

The black. The war boom caused a number of blacks to move north, looking for jobs. In the military, blacks were accepted as officer candidates, although they were trained in segregated camps. (Integration did not take place in the military until after World War II.)

The War in Europe

American Expeditionary Force. The military forces which fought in Europe, commanded by General John J. Pershing. American troops were maintained as independent units rather than filtered into the allied forces as reinforcements. This policy reflected America's isolationism.

Meuse-Argonne offensive. The greatest engagement of American troops during the war. It took place in the Argonne forest along the Meuse River from September to November 1918 and led to the Germans signing an armistice on November 11. Note the map "The Western Front, 1918" on p. 610.

The Peace

January 8, 1918: Wilson's Fourteen Points. A speech to Congress in which Wilson outlined his plans for a fair peace when the war finally ended. The plan included such points as freedom of the seas and the redrawing of boundary lines in Europe. The 14th Point called for "a general association of nations" to be established to keep the peace.

United States' delegates to the Paris Peace Conference. Wilson decided to attend the Peace Conference personally and appointed four official commissioners to accompany him: Edward House, Secretary of State Robert Lansing, General Tasker Bliss, and Henry White, a career diplomat. Other Americans went as technical advisers. Wilson erred in not appointing any Republican politicians or members of the Senate, which would have to ratify the treaty.

Big Four. Although hundreds of delegates attended the conference, most of the major decisions were made by President Wilson, Prime Minister David Lloyd George of Great Britain, Premier Georges Clemenceau of France, and Prime Minister Vittorio Orlando of Italy.

Treaty of Versailles

In June 1919, the peace treaty was signed at the Palace of Versailles, the former residence of the French monarchs. The Germans had not attended the Peace conference and were simply presented with the finished document. The treaty contained some of the following provisions.

War guilt clause. Germany had to accept responsibility for starting and perpetuating the war.

Reparations. Germany had to agree to pay compensation for damage done to civilian properties, for future pensions, and other war costs. The amount of payment was not specified in the treaty but was determined later by a Reparations Commission at $33 billion.

Mandate system. German colonies were redistributed to the Allies (with the exception of the United States) as mandates, but were theoretically under the League of Nations.

Covenant of the League of Nations. The charter of the international organization, with headquarters in Geneva, Switzerland, was part of the peace treaty. Signing the treaty automatically made a nation a member of the League.

Ratification Controversy

The Senate. Treaties must be ratified by a two-thirds vote in the Senate. Senate opposition to ratification was primarily centered around the League of Nations, and individuals were divided into three groups:

Irreconcilables. Led by the isolationist William Borah and absolutely opposed to joining the League of Nations.

"Strong" reservationists. Led by Henry Cabot Lodge, chairman of the Senate Foreign Relations Committee, who presented 14 Reservations to the League.

"Mild" reservationists. Approved the League in principle, but wanted minor alteration.

September 1919: Wilson's stroke. Wilson started a speaking tour to rally public opinion behind the League but became ill and returned to Washington where he suffered a stroke which left him partially paralyzed. Wilson was unable to lead his supporters and refused to compromise with his opponents.

Treaty rejected. Between November 1919, and March 1920, the Senate repeatedly failed to give the two-thirds vote necessary for ratification of the Treaty of Versailles. Consequently the United States did not become a member of the League of Nations. Congress formally ended the war with the Central Powers by passing a joint resolution in July 1921.

OTHER TERMS TO IDENTIFY

1914, Bryan-Chamorro Treaty. An agreement which gave the United States the option to build a canal across Nicaragua.

Venustiano Carranza (1859–1920). Mexican revolutionary who was president between 1914 and 1920 and whose forces were called the constitutionalists.

General John G. Pershing (1860–1948). Commander of the punitive expedition against Pancho Villa in Mexico (1916–1917) and of the American Expeditionary Force in Europe (1917–1918). He acquired his nickname "Black Jack" from his command of a regiment of black troops. Note the picture on p. 597.

Black Hand. A nationalistic, terrorist organization in Serbia which wanted to detach the Austro-Hungarian province of Bosnia, with Sarajevo as its capital, and join the area to Serbia. One of its members, Gavrilo Princip, assassinated Archduke Franz Ferdinand.

Louis Brandeis (1856–1941). A progressive who was the first Jew appointed to the Supreme Court, where he served as a justice from 1916 to 1939.

1916, Keating-Owen Child Labor Law. Barred goods from interstate commerce which were manufactured by children under the age of 16.

1916, Adamson Act. Established an eight-hour day for railroad workers.

Henry Cabot Lodge (1850–1924). Republican politician from Massachusetts who served in the House (1887–1893) and in the Senate (1893–1924). As chairman of the Senate Foreign Relations Committee and Senate majority leader (1918–1924), Lodge led the opposition to the Versailles Treaty and the League of Nations.

Article X of the League Covenant. Committed all League members to protect the political independence and territorial integrity of all member nations. In other words, if any member were attacked, the others would go to its aid. Many senators felt Article X interfered with Congress' authority to vote declarations of war.

GLOSSARY

"antidumping" legislation. A tariff designed to protect industry from foreign competition. In 1916 legislation was passed to prevent Europeans from "dumping" their products on the American market after the war.

consortium. An association of financial institutions or capitalists for the purpose of funding an extensive project, especially in a foreign country. President Wilson withdrew the United States' support of the international consortium that was arranging a loan to develop Chinese railroads.

contraband of war. A product which may be seized by a country at war when it is in the process of being sent to the enemy. Contraband may include everything from explosives to fabric for uniforms. In modern "total war," the list becomes almost unlimited.

diplomatic recognition. Recognizing the government of a country by establishing formal relations with it and exchanging ambassadors. For example, President Wilson refused to extend diplomatic recognition to the government of President Huerta in Mexico after Huerta had had his predecessor, Madero, shot. In another light, Wilson broke diplomatic relations with Germany in February 1917, and the German ambassador left the United States, although war was not declared until April. The absence of diplomatic recognition does not mean war; it simply indicates a severe strain in the relations between the two countries.

doughboy. The term used to refer to an American infantryman during World War I; similar to the term GI used during World War II. Doughboy was originally used in the 1850s when soldiers cleaned their white belts with a "dough" of clay.

entente. An informal agreement or understanding between two governments or groups for cooperative action. The word is French for "understanding."

hidebound. Having dry, thick skin that adheres closely to the underlying flesh, such as that of cattle. The term also means to be narrow-minded, to cling to one's own opinions and prejudices. Wilson distrusted professional diplomats, whom he thought cynical and hidebound.

imperialism. The system of expansionism involving either direct territorial acquisition of, or control over, another country.

materiel. The equipment, such as guns and ammunition, of a military force. Do not confuse materiel with the more general word material.

national self-determination. Freedom of a people to determine their own political status. The desire of various nationalities for self-determination caused the fragmentation of Austria-Hungary in 1919 into the countries of Austria, Hungary, Yugoslavia, Czechoslovakia, and Poland.

protectorate. A country which is controlled or "protected" by a more powerful country. As a result of a 1915 treaty, Haiti became a protectorate of the United States.

Round Robin. A letter or protest circulated among members of a group with comments added by each person in turn. In March 1919, Republican senators signed a Round Robin expressing opposition to the League of Nations.

ruse de guerre. A French term meaning "trick of war." For example, the *Lusitania* occasionally flew the neutral American flag rather than her own British flag as a way of deceiving German ships and submarines on the lookout for British liners.

salient. The area of a battle line, trench, fortification, or other military defense that projects closest to the enemy.

submarginal land. Infertile land with low productivity.

WORDS TO KNOW

Define the following, using the dictionary if necessary.

acrimony	prodigies
dragoon	pusillanimously
heterogeneous	reprehensible
holocaust	scurrilous
mitigation	transship

SAMPLE QUESTIONS

Multiple Choice

1. Most related to missionary diplomacy were:
   a. McKinley and Cuba.
   b. Taft and Nicaragua.
   c. Wilson and Mexico.
   d. none of the above.
2. In the Zimmermann telegram, Germany:
   a. warned the United States to stop all exports to France and Great Britain.
   b. announced a temporary pause in the submarine warfare.
   c. proposed an alliance with Mexico if the United States should enter the war.
   d. apologized for the sinking of the *Sussex*.
3. Which of the following pairs is *not* correctly matched?
   a. Bernard Baruch: War Industries Board.
   b. Henry Cabot Lodge: National War Labor Board.
   c. George Creel: Committee on Public Information.
   c. Herbert Hoover: Food Administration.
4. Which of the following was *not* included in Wilson's Fourteen Points?
   a. Alsace-Lorraine returned to France.
   b. the creation of an independent Poland.
   c. the establishment of a general association of nations.
   d. provisions for a general military buildup in Europe.
5. After World War I, the United States:
   a. formally ended the war with Germany by a joint resolution of Congress.

b. eventually ratified the Versailles Treaty.

c. never signed a peace treaty with Germany.

d. ratified both the Versailles Treaty and one of its own with Germany.

True-False

1. During Wilson's presidency, United States' troops entered the countries of Haiti, the Dominican Republic, Mexico, and Germany.
2. Wilson's winning slogan in the 1916 election was "A war to end all wars."
3. The Central Powers included Great Britain, France, and Russia.
4. Colonel Edward House was commander of the American Expeditionary Force.
5. The Sedition Act made it illegal to criticize the government of the United States.

25

The Twenties: The Aftermath of the Great War

CHRONOLOGY

1919 Eighteenth Amendment—prohibition
1920 Sacco-Vanzetti trial
1923 Teapot Dome scandal
1925 Scopes trial

CHAPTER CHECKLIST

Period of Overreaction

Red Scare. A climate of opinion in 1919–1920 in which Americans feared the growing influence of worldwide radical movements such as communism and anarchism.

A. Mitchell Palmer (1872–1936). Attorney general under Wilson who became convinced that the United States must be purged of radicals. He authorized the 1920 "Palmer raids," surprise attacks on anarchist and communist meeting places and homes conducted by Department of Justice agents. They found much inflammatory literature and very few weapons.

J. Edgar Hoover (1895–1972). The man appointed by Palmer in 1919 to head the new General Intelligence Division of the Department of Justice. He was to collect information about underground radical activities. Hoover later headed the independent Federal Bureau of Investigation.

Immigration quotas. They were designed to limit immigration based on the country of origin. They received support from labor groups which disliked job competition and from those who feared the radicals, whose membership was largely foreign. An emergency act was passed in 1921 and modified in 1924.

1929 Immigration Act. Congress allowed 150,000 immigrants a year to enter the country. The quota from each foreign country was based on the supposed origins of the entire white population of the United States in 1920. This system favored immigrants from Great Britain and northern Europe and kept out many from southern and eastern Europe.

1965 Immigration Act. An act which eliminated the national origins system. It permits 170,000 immigrants a year, admission being based on skills or occupations needed in the United States and on the need for political asylum. The law also places a limit of 120,000 on Western Hemisphere immigration, which had previously been unrestricted.

1925, Scopes trial. A trial in Tennessee which served as an example of the strength of the fundamentalist movement.

Fundamentalism. A conservative mental attitude which was prevalent in certain Protestant denominations, such as the Baptists. Fundamentalists believed in the literal truth of the Bible and rejected Darwin's theory of evolution.

1925 Tennessee law. Fundamentalist pressure caused the Tennessee legislature to pass a law forbidding instructors in state schools and colleges to teach "any theory that denies the story of the Divine Creation of man as taught in the Bible."

American Civil Liberties Union. An organization founded in 1920 which finances test cases, often to determine the validity of laws which it feels to be unconstitutional. When the ACLU learned of the Tennessee law, it offered to finance a test case if a teacher would deliberately violate the statute.

John T. Scopes. The biology teacher in Dayton, Tennessee, who was the defendant in the "Dayton Monkey Trial." The jury found him guilty of teaching evolution, and he was fined $100. The next year Scopes went to graduate school and later to South America where he worked as a geologist.

William Jennings Bryan and Clarence Darrow. Bryan, a fundamentalist who had urged passage of the law, became the state's prosecuting attorney. Darrow, a famous trial lawyer, defended Scopes.

Prohibition. The period between 1919 and 1933 during which it was illegal to manufacture, transport, or sell alcoholic beverages. Although by 1914 one quarter of the states were already dry, nationwide prohibition came about with the ratification of the Eighteenth Amendment in 1919, later repealed by the Twenty-first Amendment in 1933. The Volstead Act was the congressional measure which provided for enforcing prohibition.

Ku Klux Klan. An organization of white Protestants who actively displayed their prejudices against blacks, immigrants, Jews, and Catholics. The Klan was revived in 1915 by William J. Simmons and achieved considerable political strength in the 1920s.

Women's party. A political party founded in the 1920s when women realized that the vote had not brought them real equality. The party, led by Alice Paul, campaigned for an Equal Rights Amendment to the Constitution, but abandoned this battle by the late 1930s. An Equal Rights Amendment did pass both houses of Congress in 1972 and was submitted to the state legislatures for ratification.

Sacco-Vanzetti case. In 1920, two Italian anarchists, Nicola Sacco and Bartolomeo Vanzetti, were charged with killing two men at a Massachusetts shoe factory. After their conviction on largely circumstantial evidence, liberal supporters appealed their case, stating that prejudice had interfered with justice because the two men were immigrants and radicals. They were nonetheless electrocuted in 1927.

Literary Trends

Prewar. Writers in this period were mostly optimistic. Ezra Pound and Carl Sandburg were outstanding poets who reflected the reforming spirit of progressivism.

Postwar. Many writers became disillusioned and sharply criticized society. Intellectuals referred to themselves with self-pity as the "lost generation," and some moved to Europe, especially Paris, to write.

F. Scott Fitzgerald (1896–1940). A novelist and screenwriter who captured the fears and also the façade of gaiety of the lost generation in such works as *This Side of Paradise* (1920) and *The Great Gatsby* (1925). See the photo of Fitzgerald on p. 633.

Ernest Hemingway (1898–1961). A novelist best known for his style, suggesting powerful emotions and actions with direct, simple wording. Two of his best-selling novels were *The Sun Also Rises* (1926) and *A Farewell to Arms* (1929). Note the picture of Hemingway on p. 633.

H. L. Mencken (1880–1956). Founder and editor of the *American Mercury,* a widely read 1920s magazine which specialized in witty denunciations of almost everything. Mencken's criticisms were cynical and amusing rather than constructive.

Sinclair Lewis (1885–1951). A novelist whose best works portrayed life in a small midwestern town in the 1920s. *Main Street* (1920) was an exposé of such a town, and *Babbitt* (1922) described a middle-class businessman of the Midwest.

The Black

Harlem. A residential section of New York City which was predominantly white and middle-class as late as 1910 and then rapidly became populated by blacks. In the 1920s it was the cultural capital of American blacks, the center of the "Harlem Renaissance," a flourishing of black writers, musicians, newspapers, magazines, theatrical companies, and libraries.

Marcus Garvey (1887–1940). A Jamaican who founded the Universal

Negro Improvement Association and moved its headquarters to Harlem in 1916. Garvey encouraged blacks to move to Africa and set up the Black Star Line Steamship Company to transport them. The line went bankrupt in 1923, and Garvey was imprisoned for having defrauded thousands who had invested in its stock.

WARREN GAMALIEL HARDING (1865–1923), 29th President

Born in Ohio; attended Ohio Central College; and became publisher of a newspaper, the Marion *Star*.
Republican member of the state legislature and a lieutenant governor of Ohio.
United States senator (1915–1921).
President (1921–1923).
Died of a heart attack, succeeded by Vice-president Calvin Coolidge.

Harding's Era of Normalcy

Andrew Mellon (1855–1937). A Pennsylvania banker and aluminum industry owner who served as secretary of the treasury from 1921 to 1932. Mellon's policies included lowering the taxes of the rich so that they could invest their money in other businesses. He also wanted to raise tariff duties, a measure which was bitterly opposed by the "Farm Bloc," a combination of middle-western Republicans and southern Democrats who tried to unite agriculture against the business interests. Finally, Mellon was committed to balancing the budget and reducing the national debt from the war by cutting expenses and administering the government more efficiently.

Scandals. Harding's administration was riddled with scandals, not committed by Harding himself but by the "Ohio Gang." When discovered, some received prison sentences; others committed suicide. One example was *Charles R. Forbes* of the Veterans Bureau, who took millions of dollars which had been appropriated for the construction of veterans' hospitals. Forbes was sentenced to two years in prison.

Albert B. Fall and the Teapot Dome scandal. Secretary of the Interior Fall leased government-owned oil reserves to private oil companies, one of which was the Teapot Dome reserve in Wyoming which was turned over to Harry Sinclair's Mammouth Oil Company. Conservationists protested that the oil reserves should be preserved for future naval use, and in 1923 a Senate investigation began. It was discovered that Fall had received large bribes from oil companies to lease the land, including $300,000 from Sinclair. Eventually Sinclair and Fall received jail sentences.

CALVIN COOLIDGE (1872–1933), 30th President

Born in Vermont; graduated from Amherst; and remained in Massachusetts to practice law.

Republican governor of Massachusetts, who became popular among conservatives because of his use of the militia in suppressing the 1919 Boston Police Strike.

Vice-president of the United States (1921–1923).

President (1923–1929).

Coolidge Prosperity

Henry Ford (1863–1947). A Michigan manufacturer who was largely responsible for the growth of the automobile industry. Ford had two important insights. The first was an emphasis on mass production, so as to bring car prices within the range of the ordinary citizen. Mass production was made possible through his introduction of the Ford moving assembly line, which carried the parts to the worker. Second, Ford believed in paying high wages as a means of stimulating output and slowing down the turnover of workers. Ford produced the Model T from 1909 to 1927, and then retooled for the Model A. Today the company produces many models and is run by Ford's grandson, Henry Ford II.

Trade associations. Voluntary organizations formed by producers in various industries to exchange information, discuss policies toward government and the public, and set prices. Rather than the government regulating business in the 1920s, industries "regulated" their own competition.

George Peek. An Illinois plow manufacturer who suggested a plan to help agriculture, which was not doing as well as other parts of the economy. Peek suggested that the government buy up surplus wheat, cotton, and other staples, which would cause domestic prices to rise. Then the government could sell the surpluses abroad at the lower world price, recovering its losses by assessing an "equalization fee" on American farmers. The plan had flaws, but Farm Bloc congressmen took it up and pushed through laws in 1927 and in 1928, both of which were vetoed by Coolidge, who felt the government should not tamper with the economy.

"Big bull market." The rapidly rising stock market in the late 1920s. Much money was invested in speculative ventures rather than in sound companies. A bull market is characterized by rising prices, whereas a bear market means falling prices. A bull throws its victim upward on its horns, a bear pulls its victim down and paws it underfoot.

OTHER TERMS TO IDENTIFY

Plumb Plan. A proposal at the end of World War I to continue government operation of the railroad system. It was rejected, and the lines returned to private control.

Imagism. A type of poetry developed by Ezra Pound and others which did away with abstract generalizations and concentrated upon concrete word pictures to convey meaning.

Henry Adams (1838–1918). A writer and historian who in his autobiography, *The Education of Henry Adams* (1918), warned that industrialism was crushing the human spirit. Adams' disillusionment was picked up by the "lost generation" of the 1920s.

Langston Hughes (1902–1967). A poet who was one of the main figures of the Harlem Renaissance.

Ohio Gang. Personal friends of President Harding who received political appointments, some of them to lesser offices, others to more important posts, such as Harry Daugherty, Harding's attorney general.

Alfred E. Smith (1873–1944). Progressive governor of New York who was the Democratic presidential candidate in 1928. Smith was defeated by Herbert Hoover because of his Catholicism, his big-city origins, and his stand against Prohibition.

GLOSSARY

abstinence. The practice of voluntarily denying oneself alcoholic beverages. Temperance is another word which means "to abstain from alcoholic liquors." The temperance movement eventually led to nationwide prohibition, which means it was illegal to make or sell alcoholic drinks.

amending the Constitution. To change the Constitution permanently requires a two-thirds vote in each house of Congress and ratification by three-fourths of the states.

anti-Semitism. Hostility toward or prejudice against Jews. Henry Ford engaged in anti-Semitic propaganda in his newspaper, the Dearborn *Independent*.

ballistics. The science which studies the motion of projectiles or bullets shot from artillery or firearms. Modern ballistic studies of Nicola Sacco's gun have shown that he, at least, was probably guilty as charged.

Bohemian. A person with literary or artistic interests who disregards conventional standards of behavior. The term was derived from the belief that gypsies originally came from Bohemia, a province in Czechoslovakia. During the early 1900s, New York's Greenwich Village teemed with youthful Bohemians.

Bolshevist. A participant in the Russian Revolution who followed Lenin's leadership and favored a more revolutionary Marxism. By 1919 the Bolshevists called themselves communists.

bootlegger. A person who made, sold, or transported alcoholic liquor illegally. The name was derived from the smugglers' practice of carrying liquor in the legs of tall boots.

cause célèbre. A French term meaning "a famous or celebrated legal case." The Sacco-Vanzetti case became a *cause célèbre* in the 1920s.

Sigmund Freud (1856–1939). The Austrian physician who is considered the founder of psychoanalysis. Freud's theories included such concepts as the influence of the unconscious and of sexuality on human psychology. Freud's ideas had a profound effect on the intellectuals of the 1920s.

hara-kiri. Ritual suicide by disembowelment as formerly practiced by the Japanese upper classes. One commentator of the 1920s stated that the Federal Trade Commission of that period seemed to be trying to commit hara-kiri. He meant that big businessmen had been appointed to the commission, and then they were supposed to restrict and regulate monopolies, in a sense, cutting themselves open.

iconoclasm. Attacking or overthrowing established institutions, actions, or attitudes. The 1920s reflected a shift from faith in the old order to iconoclasm.

King James translation of the Bible. The translation from Hebrew and Greek into English published in 1611 while James I was King of England.

May Day. The first day of May. In Germany, Russia, and several other European countries, May Day was celebrated as Labor Day. In 1920 Attorney General Palmer feared that radicals were planning terroristic demonstrations on May Day, but they did not occur and the Red Scare subsided.

oligopoly. Control by a few competing sellers of the amount and price of a given product; a shared monopoly. "Regulated" competition and oligopoly were typical of the 1920s.

philistinism. Smug conventionality. A philistine is one who is indifferent or antagonistic to cultural and artistic values. The philistinism of the dull politicians of the 1920s turned many intellectuals into sharp critics of society.

ptomaine poisoning. Illness caused by bacterial poisons in spoiled foods. In 1923 Harding's physician diagnosed his illness as ptomaine poisoning from having eaten a tainted Japanese crab. Actually Harding had had a heart attack, and after briefly rallying he died on August 2.

quartier latin. The area in Paris along the left bank of the Seine River where a number of artists and writers lived. It was called the Latin Quarter because during the Middle Ages it was the section where students lived, and at that time all courses were conducted in Latin.

West Indian. A person from the West Indies, the chain of islands which separates the Caribbean Sea from the Atlantic Ocean. Marcus Garvey was a West Indian from the island of Jamaica.

scapegoat. A person or group bearing blame for others. The term is from a Biblical account in Leviticus in which a live goat over whose head Aaron confessed all of the sins of the children of Israel was sent into the wilderness, symbolically bearing their sins. The Ku Klux Klan used immigrants, Jews, and Catholics as scapegoats, feeling that if they were driven away, some of the problems of a changing America would also disappear.

speakeasy. A "secret" bar or saloon where alcoholic drinks were illegally sold during the Prohibition era.

xenophobia. An undue contempt or fear of foreigners.

WORDS TO KNOW

Define the following, using the dictionary if necessary.

antedeluvian	maudlin
deleterious	meretricious
effete	posthumously
libertines	verisimilitude

SAMPLE QUESTIONS

Multiple Choice

1. A cause for the rise of organized crime in the 1920s:
   a. stock market speculation.
   b. nonenforcement of antitrust laws.
   c. corruption in the Harding Administration.
   d. Prohibition.
2. One manifestation of the fundamentalist movement in the 1920s:
   a. growing concentration of wealth.
   b. jazz.
   c. speakeasies.
   d. the Scopes trial.
3. Which of the following phrases is most associated with the Republican candidate for the presidency in 1920?
   a. "return to normalcy."
   b. "every man deserves a square deal."
   c. "the golden twenties."
   d. "business as usual."
4. The secretary of interior under Harding who accepted bribes to transfer federal oil lands to oil companies was:
   a. Charles Forbes.

   b. Harry Daugherty.

   c. Albert Fall.

   d. Andrew Mellon.

5. During the 1920s appointments to federal regulatory agencies such as the Interstate Commerce Commission and the Federal Reserve Board were generally:

   a. liberal.

   b. pro-big business.

   c. radical.

   d. anti-big business.

True-False

1. A. Mitchell Palmer was secretary of the treasury during the 1920s.
2. The immigration quota system discriminated against southern and eastern Europeans.
3. The intellectuals of the 1920s sometimes referred to themselves as the "lost generation."
4. Marcus Garvey wanted to set up a separate black state within the United States.
5. Henry Ford dominated the automobile industry by annually introducing new models.

26

The Great Depression
1929-1939

CHRONOLOGY

1929   Stock market crash
1932   Bonus Army march on Washington, D.C.
1933   National Industrial Recovery Act.
1933   Agricultural Adjustment Act
1933   Tennessee Valley Authority
1933   Federal Deposit Insurance Corporation
1935   Works Progress Administration
1935   National Labor Relations Act
1935   Social Security Act
1935   CIO founded

CHAPTER CHECKLIST

HERBERT HOOVER (1874–1964), 31st President

Born in Iowa and graduated from Stanford University in California.
Became a millionaire as a mining engineer.
Headed the Federal Food Administration during World War I.
Secretary of commerce (1921–1928).
President (1929–1933).

Hoover and the Depression

Hoover's program
Cooperative action by businessmen to maintain prices and wages.
More public works programs.

Lower interest rates.

Federal loans to failing banks and industries.

Aid to homeowners unable to make mortgage payments.

Government support of cooperative farm marketing schemes.

Problems with the program

No production control or acreage allotments for farm products.

Authority remained with the sometimes inefficient state and local agencies rather than shifting to the federal government.

No federal funds for the relief of individuals.

Importance of balancing budget overemphasized.

Duties on most manufactured products raised by the 1930 Hawley-Smoot Tariff.

Hooversvilles. Ramshackle communities which grew up on vacant lots and in garbage dumps during the depression. The jobless and the homeless constructed houses out of packing boxes and rusty sheet metal. The nickname blamed Hoover for the economic situation.

Bonus Army. Some unemployed World War I veterans marched to Washington in the summer of 1932 to demand the immediate payment of their bonuses for wartime service, not due until 1945. After Congress rejected their appeal, most left, but around 2,000 remained and camped out at Anacostia Flats on the Potomac River. After disturbances, President Hoover ordered troops under General Douglas MacArthur to clear them out, which they did, using fixed bayonets and tanks.

FRANKLIN DELANO ROOSEVELT (1882–1945), 32nd President

Born in New York and graduated from Harvard.

Married his distant cousin, Eleanor, niece of Theodore Roosevelt.

Served in the New York legislature and as assistant secretary of the Navy.

Unsuccessful Democratic vice-presidential candidate in 1920.

Had infantile paralysis, or polio, in 1921, which left him badly crippled.

Governor of New York (1929–1933).

President (1933–1945).

Died after beginning his fourth term in office, and was succeeded by Vice-president Harry Truman.

Roosevelt and the New Deal

New Deal. The label given by President Roosevelt to his domestic program of relief, recovery, and reform during the depression. He used the term when, breaking precedent, he flew to Chicago to give his acceptance speech personally at the 1932 Democratic convention. "I pledge you, I pledge myself, to a new deal for the American people," he declared.

Hundred days. The early weeks of the New Deal from March to June 1933, in which Congress passed a number of proposals made by Roosevelt to revive the economy. Some of the laws set up "alphabetical agencies" to administer the program.

National Industrial Recovery Act (NIRA). A law which permitted manufacturers to draw up industry-wide codes of fair business practices in order to raise prices and limit production by agreement. The act also created the National Recovery Administration, headed by General Hugh Johnson, to supervise the business codes. The NIRA provided minimum-wage and maximum-hour regulations and guaranteed workers the right to form unions and bargain collectively. In addition, it established the Public Works Administration with authority to spend $3.3 billion on roads and public buildings. The Supreme Court ruled the NIRA unconstitutional in *Schechter* v. *U.S.* (1935).

Agricultural Adjustment Act. An act designed to curtail production of farm products in order to raise prices. The first year farmers were paid to slaughter animals and to plow under crops, actions not easily understood by hungry Americans at that time. Thereafter, a limit on the number of acres which could be planted in a particular crop was sufficient. In addition, farmers received "rental" payments for withdrawing part of their land from cultivation. These programs were administered by the Agricultural Adjustment Administration (AAA). The objective was to lift agriculture prices to "parity," that is, to be on a par with industrial prices. The period 1909–1914 was viewed as a prosperous time for farmers, so that era was used as a basis for comparison. For example, after comparing the price of cotton with the price of steel in 1909–1914, the AAA could determine how much the price of cotton needed to be raised in 1933.

The AAA was declared unconstitutional by *U.S.* v. *Butler* in 1936, but a modified AAA was established in 1938 and became the basis for farm support programs which continued after the New Deal.

Tennessee Valley Authority (TVA). A three-person board was authorized by law to build dams, power plants, and transmission lines and sell electricity and fertilizer throughout the seven-state region of the Tennessee River basin. The board could also undertake flood control, soil conservation, and restoration projects and improve navigation. The regional planning project was pushed by Senator George Norris of Nebraska and opposed by private power companies which feared the competitive rates and claimed it was a sign of creeping socialism. The TVA still exists.

Works Progress Administration (WPA). A federal agency under Harry Hopkins which spent $11 billion and found employment for 8.5 million people between 1935 and 1943. Its purpose was to give people jobs instead of money handouts. In addition to an extensive public works program, the WPA also developed the Federal Theater Project, the Federal Writers' Project, and the Federal Art Project, so that a wide variety of unemployed people could work. Some felt, however, that the WPA did not spend enough. Note the chart entitled "Unemployment, 1929–1941" on p. 661.

Intellectuals and the New Deal

"Brain Trust." A group of unofficial advisers to Roosevelt, many of them recruited from the faculty of Columbia University in New York. The group was headed by Raymond Moley, a Columbia political scientist, who encouraged close cooperation between government and the business community.

John Maynard Keynes (1883–1946). A British economist whose ideas about combatting the depression were influential among some members of the Roosevelt administration. Roosevelt had met Keynes in 1934 and was not too impressed; only necessity forced him to adopt a partially Keynesian approach. Keynes advocated monetary expansion, that is, getting money into the hands of the people who will immediately spend it, such as through relief programs or old-age pensions. Another way of fighting the depression, according to Keynes, was through deficit financing, that is, putting money into the economy through government spending, rather than concentrating on balancing the budget. To see how deficit financing was practiced in the United States, note the chart entitled "The Federal Budget, 1929–1941" on p. 665.

Extremists Who Opposed the New Deal

Huey Long (1893–1935). A Louisiana politician who became governor in 1928 and senator in 1930. At first he supported his fellow Democrat, Roosevelt, but by 1935 he headed a national "Share-Our-Wealth" movement, and planned to form a third party. His program was designed to take money from the very wealthy and give it to the very poor. Long wanted the government to confiscate all family fortunes of more than $5 million and to place a 100 percent tax on income over $1 million a year. The money thus collected would be used to provide every family with a "homestead," an annual income of $2,000–3,000, plus pensions and education benefits. Long was killed by an assassin in 1935, but his popularity may have pushed Roosevelt to more liberal programs. Note the photograph on p. 662.

Father Charles E. Coughlin (1891–   ). A Catholic priest who became well known through a weekly radio program. Coughlin's programs shifted from religion to politics, and by 1935 he was an active critic of the New Deal, claiming that the only way to correct the economy was through drastic inflation. Coughlin's National Union for Social Justice appealed especially to lower-middle-class urban dwellers, who contributed hundreds of thousands of dollars to his organization. By 1939 Coughlin was pro-Nazi and formed a fascist organization called the Christian Front. See his photo on p. 662.

Dr. Francis E. Townsend (1867–1960). A California physician who campaigned for "Old-Age Revolving Pensions." He felt the government should pay all unemployed persons 60 or over a pension of $200 a month with the condition that they spend the entire sum within 30 days. The elderly formed Townsend Clubs, and the *Townsend National Weekly* reached a circulation of over 200,000. The Townsend plan was never adopted, but in 1935 the Social Security Act was enacted to relieve partially the plight of the elderly.

Second New Deal

A period in 1935, sometimes called the Second Hundred Days, in which the new Congress (members of the House of Representatives are elected every two years) passed a large number of laws to deal with the depression.

National Labor Relations Act. An act promoted by Senator Robert Wagner, and sometimes called the Wagner Act, which restored the labor guarantees that had been voided when the National Industrial Recovery Act was declared unconstitutional. The act gave workers the right to bargain collectively and prohibited employers from interfering with union organization. It also established the National Labor Relations Board (NLRB) to investigate employer practices. This act was very effective in making labor more powerful.

Social Security Act. An act which set up retirement pensions and unemployment compensation. There were also provisions for financial assistance to the handicapped, widows, and dependent children. Money for the program was contributed partly by the employee and partly by the employer, and the size of the pension was dependent on the amount earned by the worker.

Rural Electrification Administration. An agency created by an executive order, not by an act of Congress, to help rural areas finance electrification. The REA was authorized to lend money at low interest rates to private utility companies and to farmer cooperatives and was very successful in accomplishing its goal. In 1935, 10 percent of American farms had electricity; by 1950, 90 percent did.

Supreme Court

A majority of the Supreme Court justices during Roosevelt's first term were wary of the trend toward increasing the power of the government as a means of coping with the depression and, as a consequence, declared several acts unconstitutional. In 1936 Roosevelt unsuccessfully tried to "reform" the Court. After that struggle, several conservatives modified their position, and others resigned, permitting Roosevelt to appoint justices sympathetic with his views.

"Court-packing" bill. A bill proposed by Roosevelt in 1936 which was not passed by Congress. Under this proposal, a 70-year-old member of the

Supreme Court had the option of retiring with full pay. If he chose not to retire, the president could appoint an additional justice, up to a maximum of six, to ease the burden of work. In making this proposal, Roosevelt misjudged the climate of opinion of the Congress and the country. Vocal opposition forced him to abandon his plan in 1937, and Roosevelt's prestige never fully recovered.

Significance of the New Deal

As a result of this program, the country was committed to the idea that the federal government should accept responsibility for the welfare of the nation and of its people. New Deal decisions led to many changes:

Regulated previously uncontrolled areas, such as the stock exchange, agriculture, labor relations, and relief for the needy.

Effected changes which prevented later economic declines from becoming Great Depressions (FDIC and Federal Securities Act).

Helped workers obtain a larger share of the profits of industry (NLRB).

Checked the decline of the agricultural classes (AAA).

Eased the economic impact of old age and unemployment (Social Security).

Switched many black voters from the Republican to the Democratic party.

Brought electricity to farms (REA).

Rehabilitated slums through urban public housing projects.

Built dams to provide electrical power (TVA).

Brought art and theater to millions (WPA programs).

OTHER TERMS TO IDENTIFY

1932, Reconstruction Finance Corporation. An agency established by the Hoover administration to make loans to banks, railroads, and insurance companies. This action was an important step in the extension of federal authority in the economic sphere, but in keeping with Hoover's philosophy, the transactions were loans, not gifts.

Farm Holiday movements. Demonstrations by farmers, particularly in midwestern states, who felt frustrated by the falling price spiral of their produce. Many farmers refused to send their crops to market in protest against 31-cents-a-bushel corn and burned the corn for fuel instead. Farmers also blocked roads and rail lines, dumped milk, overturned trucks, and established picket lines to enforce their boycott, hoping that prices would go up.

1933, Twentieth Amendment. A Constitutional amendment which advanced the date of the president's inauguration from March 4 to January 20. In addition, the amendment provided for new Congresses to convene in January instead of the following December. This portion did away with "lame duck" Congresses in which the holdover congressmen, some of whom had not been reelected, did not always work enthusiastically with the new president.

1933, Federal Deposit Insurance Corporation (FDIC). An agency chartered to insure deposits up to a fixed sum in member banks of the Federal Reserve System. Originally the FDIC guaranteed deposits up to $2,500; the guarantee has since been raised to $20,000. The purpose of the FDIC was to restore confidence in banks after the closing of so many during the early 1930s.

Congress of Industrial Organizations. In 1935 when the American Federation of Labor continued to show little interest in unskilled, mass-production workers, *John L. Lewis* of the United Mine Workers formed the Committee for Industrial Organization and tried to organize these laborers into industrial unions. In 1937 these unions were expelled from the AFL, and the following year they formed the Congress of Industrial Organizations, successfully organizing such industries as steel, automobiles, rubber, textiles, and shipbuilding. In 1955 the CIO merged with the AFL.

1934, Federal Housing Administration. A federal agency which made available low-cost, long-term loans to stimulate the building and improvement of private homes. The FHA brought recovery to the housebuilding industry and survives today as an important agency.

"Sit-down strikes." A series of strikes took place in a number of industries in 1937, beginning at the General Motors' plant in Michigan. The striking workers barricaded themselves inside the factories, rather than staying out. The purpose was to prevent continued plant operations with scab labor, that is, strikebreakers. The government did not intervene in these strikes, and the employers, fearful for their expensive equipment, soon gave in to the workers' demands. However, the seizure of property and the occasional violence alarmed many moderates, and their sympathy for labor reform began to cool.

"Roosevelt recession." A period beginning in August 1937, in which the economy suffered a sharp decline. In June of 1937 President Roosevelt ordered a cutback on relief programs, and the results were disastrous. Stocks fell in value; unemployment rose by 2 million; and industrial production slumped. Roosevelt hoped that the economy would right itself, but by April 1938, he reconsidered and encouraged massive government spending once again.

1938, Commodity Credit Corporation. An agency under the new AAA program which was authorized to lend money to farmers, using their surplus crops as collateral. The surpluses were stored by the government, and when prices rose, the farmer could then sell his produce, repay the loan, and hopefully have money left over. This measure was similar to the subtreasury scheme suggested by the Populists in the 1890s.

1938, Fair Labor Standards Act. An act which set minimum wages and maximum working hours for industries involved in interstate commerce. The act also established time-and-a-half pay for overtime and forbade child labor on products shipped interstate. This law has continued to be important as new classes of workers have been brought within its protection and minimum wages increased.

GLOSSARY

Hugo Black (1886–1971). Democratic senator from Alabama (1927–1937) who was appointed to the Supreme Court (1937–1971) by President Roosevelt. Black was known for his liberal views concerning protection of individual rights.

boondoggles. A critical term applied by New Deal opponents to the supposedly useless public works programs of the 1930s.

classical economics. The theory that the economy will naturally have ups and downs and that the business community should simply wait it out without the government interfering, that is, adopt a laissez-faire attitude. Some of the programs recommended by President Hoover, such as the Reconstruction Finance Corporation, illustrated that he rejected classical economics.

cracker-barrel. Resembling or characteristic of the informal discussions of people who used to hang around the general store in a small town. Cracker-barrels were common fixtures in country stores.

fireside chats. Informal radio talks by President Franklin Roosevelt. They were used to establish rapport with the public and to help the people understand Roosevelt's plans and policies, both during the depression and the war.

jerry-built. Shoddily or cheaply constructed. The Bonus Army settled down with their families in a jerry-built camp of shacks and tents.

Lilliputian. One of the tiny, six-inches-tall inhabitants of Lilliput, an imaginary island in Jonathan Swift's *Gulliver's Travels*.

moratorium. An authorization to a debtor to suspend payments temporarily. In 1931 President Hoover proposed a one-year moratorium on all international obligations such as war debts and reparations.

multiplier industry. An industry which causes a number of related businesses to develop. Automobile manufacturing was the great multiplier industry of the 1920s and fostered such businesses as road construction and gas stations.

pink campuses. A term referring to college campuses used by those who felt many college professors and students were communist sympathizers. These right-wing individuals did not necessarily believe that the campuses were full of reds, that is, full-fledged communist revolutionaries, but at least "pinkos" could be found. In 1936 Gerald L. K. Smith, who took over Huey Long's organization, stated that the New Deal was led by "a

slimy group of men culled from the pink campuses of America.'' He was
referring to President Roosevelt's Brain Trust.

underconsumption. Consumers not buying enough products to keep the
economy moving. When inventories piled up, manufacturers closed down
plants and laid off workers, who consequently had less money to spend.
In general, during the 1920s the average worker was not making enough
money to buy the products being manufactured, which led to underconsumption.

WORDS TO KNOW

Define the following, using the dictionary if necessary.

aegis	internecine
collateral	mellifluous
élan	nadir
geneticist	orotund
inimitable	vicissitudes

SAMPLE QUESTIONS

Multiple Choice

1. The New Deal philosophy toward relief could be best summarized by
   which of the following:
   a. Relief should be handled primarily by private agencies such as re-
      ligious and charitable organizations.
   b. Local municipalities should finance and administer their own pro-
      grams.
   c. The "dole" is preferable to work relief.
   d. Work relief as recommended by Harry Hopkins is preferable to the
      "dole" since it preserves self-respect and technical skills of the re-
      cipient.
2. The Tennessee Valley Authority was the following *except one:*
   a. branded by critics as socialism.
   b. promoted by Senator Norris.
   c. one of the least successful of the New Deal schemes.
   d. partially established a "yardstick" to measure electrical rates.
3. A New Deal program that put large numbers of painters, musicians,
   and actors to work was the:
   a. Works Progress Administration.
   b. Public Works Administration.
   c. National Youth Administration.
   d. Civilian Conservation Corps.

4. Labor was guaranteed its right to organize and bargain collectively by:
   a. the Clayton Act.
   b. the Bonus Army.
   c. the Wagner Act.
   d. the Taft-Hartley Act.
5. Which one of the following was *not* a reason why President Roosevelt attempted to enlarge the Supreme Court?
   a. Most of the nine justices had been selected by Republican presidents and reflected another philosophy.
   b. Roosevelt felt that the "nine old men" on the Court were holding up progress.
   c. Roosevelt felt he had a mandate from the people after the 1936 election.
   d. The majority of the Supreme Court believed in a "loose construction" of the Constitution.

True-False

1. President Hoover preferred local control of relief programs when possible.
2. The Bonus Army was a veterans' organization which favored Huey Long's "share-our-wealth" program.
3. John Maynard Keynes was a Columbia professor who headed the Brain Trust.
4. Members of Townsend Clubs were more interested in the Social Security Act than in the Civilian Conservation Corps.
5. The AAA and the REA were designed to help the same type of worker.

ANSWERS
Multiple Choice: d, c, a, c, d. True-False: T, F, F, T, T.

27

Isolationism and War 1921-1945

CHRONOLOGY

1921–1922   Washington Armament Conference
1928   Kellogg-Briand Pact
1932   Stimson Doctrine
1934–1936   Nye Committee investigation
1940   Destroyers-for-bases deal
1941   Lend-Lease Act
1941   Pearl Harbor, Hawaii, attacked
1944   D-Day in France
1945   War ended in Europe and the Pacific

CHAPTER CHECKLIST

Isolationism

Isolationism. The traditional foreign policy of the United States that was briefly interrupted by World War I but reemerged in the 1920s. In general, this policy reflected the opinion of Americans who feared "entanglements" might lead to another war.

1921–1922, Washington Armament Conference. Talks held in Washington, D.C., to discuss disarmament and the problems of the Far East. A number of agreements were signed by the nations involved.

Four-Power Treaty. An agreement signed by the United States, Great Britain, Japan, and France which committed these nations to respect one another's interests in the Pacific Ocean and to confer in case any other power launched an attack there. However, they only agreed to consult and made no promises to help one another.

Five-Power Treaty. An agreement signed by the four powers plus Italy which committed them to stop building battleships for ten years and to reduce their fleets of capital, or large, ships on a fixed ratio. However, nothing was said about cruisers or other warships, or about land and air forces.

Nine-Power Treaty. An agreement signed by all the nations at the conference in which they agreed to respect China's independence and maintain the Open Door, that is, equal trading opportunities for all countries. Actually, none of the powers with spheres of influence in China had any intentions of giving up its special privileges.

1928, Kellogg-Briand Pact. An agreement negotiated by diplomats of 15 nations in Paris and later supported by over 60 nations, which condemned war as an instrument of foreign policy. Making war illegal, however, proved difficult to enforce. The pact was named after United States Secretary of State Frank Kellogg and French Foreign Minister Aristide Briand.

Good Neighbor Policy. The western hemispheric policy started by Herbert Hoover and usually associated with Franklin Roosevelt. Primarily it marked a withdrawal from the policy of intervention, often with troops, in the countries of Latin America. Marines were recalled from Haiti, the Dominican Republic, and Nicaragua, and the Platt Amendment to the Cuban Constitution was abrogated, or formally abolished.

1930, Clark Memorandum. A policy statement by Undersecretary of State Reuben Clark which disavowed the Roosevelt Corollary to the Monroe Doctrine. It reaffirmed the Monroe Doctrine's principle of the United States' "right" to keep other nations out of the hemisphere but added that the principle did not give us the right to intervene ourselves, unless it were a matter of self-preservation.

1933, Montevideo Pan-American Conference. A hemispheric meeting in Uruguay in which a resolution was passed stating that "no state has the right to intervene in the internal or external affairs of another." The United States was represented by Roosevelt's secretary of state, Cordell Hull, who voted for the resolution.

Totalitarianism

Totalitarianism. A political, economic, and ideological system involving complete subordination of the individual to the state and the concentration of political power in the hands of a dictator. Military control in Japan, fascism in Italy, Nazism in Germany, and communism in the Soviet Union were all examples of totalitarian governments.

Japan. The emperor was dominated by military leaders with expansionist goals.

1932, Stimson Doctrine. A policy set forth by Secretary of State Henry Stimson which stated that the United States would not recognize territories acquired by aggression. The doctrine specifically referred to Japan's 1931 invasion of Chinese Manchuria, which was converted into a puppet state called Manchukuo. The Stimson Doctrine said the United States would not recognize the legality of territorial seizures made in violation of American treaty rights and that such action violated the Kellogg-Briand and the Nine-Power pacts. However the protest was toothless, and Japan proceeded with her expansionist policies to create a Greater East Asia Co-Prosperity Sphere.

Italy. The king appointed Benito Mussolini (1883–1945) as premier in 1922, and Italy embarked on a domestic program of dictatorial socialism called fascism and of foreign expansion into Ethiopia and Albania.

Fascism. A philosophy or system of government in which there was a merging of governmental and business leadership, so that the planned economy would help the aggressive foreign policies of the government. Characteristics of fascism included extreme nationalism and a hatred of socialists and communists. Fascism did not start as a well-defined theory but was developed through the years by Mussolini. The term referred to the *fasces* of the ancient Roman empire, a symbol of governmental authority consisting of a bundle of rods bound around an ax.

Germany. A republic which named Adolf Hitler (1889–1945) as chancellor in 1933.

Nazism. The ideology and movement also called "National Socialism" which directed Germany from 1933 to 1945. The movement emphasized state control of the economy and territorial expansion. It also stressed the alleged racial superiority of the German people and used the Jews and communists as scapegoats.

Money

War debts. During and after World War I the United States loaned over $10 billion to its military allies for munitions and other supplies. Repayment of the sum was almost impossible and caused resentment on both sides.

Reparations. Money to be paid by Germany to the World War I victors. The United States demanded none. The reparations amounted to $33 billion, and European nations were depending on that money to rebuild their economies and to obtain the international exchange needed to pay their war debts to the United States. Neither the war debts nor the reparations were ever paid in full.

1924, Dawes Plan. An international agreement worked out by a committee headed by the financier Charles Dawes. Under this plan Germany received a loan of $200 million to stabilize its currency and slow the rapid inflation of the mark, the German currency. The plan avoided setting a grand total of reparation payments and instead scheduled annual payments of $250 million a year.

1929, Young Plan. An agreement which scaled down the total reparations payment to $8 billion. The plan was drawn up by the financier Owen Young. The payments were not completed.

1931, one-year moratorium. Hoover helped arrange a suspension of all international obligations, and payments were never really resumed.

1934, Johnson Debt Default Act. An act of Congress which banned further loans to nations that had not paid their war debts.

1934–1936, Nye Committee Report. The outcome of a Senate investigation headed by isolationist Gerald P. Nye of North Dakota. It stated that bankers and munitions manufacturers, referred to as "merchants of death," had pulled the United States into World War I in order to protect their investments. Although Nye's claims were exaggerated and in some cases inaccurate, they reflected the isolationist tenor of the times and led to legislation designed to prevent a repeat performance.

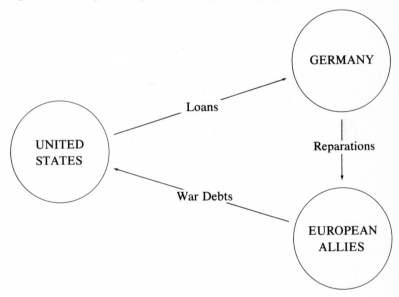

Neutrality

1935, Neutrality Act. An act which forbade the sale of munitions to all belligerents, that is, countries involved in war, whenever the president proclaimed that a state of war existed. It also stated that Americans who traveled on belligerent ships did so at their own risk. Both provisions were designed to prevent pre-World War I problems. They were first invoked after Italy invaded Ethiopia in 1935.

1936, Neutrality Act. An act forbidding all loans to belligerents.

1936, Neutrality Act. An act which broadened the arms embargo to cover civil wars and was applied to the Spanish Civil War, which raged from 1936 to 1939.

1937, Neutrality Act. A law which continued the embargo on munitions and loans, forbade Americans to travel on belligerent ships, and gave the president the authority to place the sale of other goods to belligerents on a cash-and-carry basis.

1938, Munich Conference. A meeting in Munich, Germany, attended by

Germany's Hitler, Italy's Mussolini, British Prime Minister Neville Chamberlain, and French Premier Edouard Daladier to discuss the fate of the Sudetenland region in Czechoslovakia. Hitler maintained that the German-speaking inhabitants of the province should be part of Germany and that this was the last territorial acquisition that he planned to make. The other powers agreed to the takeover; that is, they followed a policy of appeasement. The next spring, however, Hitler seized the rest of Czechoslovakia.

1939, Neutrality Act. An act pushed through by the Democratic majority in Congress which permitted the sale of arms and other contraband on a cash-and-carry basis. Short-term loans were also authorized, but none of the goods sold to belligerents could be carried in American ships. Hopefully this measure would prevent United States ships from being torpedoed by German submarines. At the same time, it helped the Allies, who had a naval superiority in the Atlantic.

1940, Destroyers-for-bases deal. An executive agreement in which the British received 50 American destroyers in exchange for six naval bases on British possessions in the Caribbean. In addition, the United States leased bases in Bermuda and Newfoundland. The major purpose of the exchange was to save Great Britain, which was the only European country still successfully resisting German advances. At the same time the United States received important outposts to protect the Atlantic seaboard.

1941, Lend-Lease Act. An act authorizing the expenditure of $7 million for war materials that the president could sell, lend, lease, exchange, or transfer to any country whose defense he felt was vital to that of the United States. As a result, the United States became "the arsenal of democracy" in order to save Great Britain. Americans were willing to give all aid short of war.

1941, Pearl Harbor. In a surprise attack on December 7, the Japanese bombed the United States naval base at Pearl Harbor, Hawaii, causing great destruction to the Pacific Fleet. The following day Congress declared war on Japan. On December 11 Germany and Italy honored the Rome-Berlin-Tokyo Axis agreement and declared war on the United States.

Home Front During the War

Roosevelt's basic decisions
To pay a large part of the cost of war by taxing rather than by borrowing.

To ration scarce raw materials and consumer goods.

To treat minority groups and opposition elements fairly.

Economy
Office of War Mobilization. A wartime board which controlled priorities and prices. James Byrnes was the "economic czar" at its

head. Rents, food prices, and wages were regulated; consumer items were rationed; and by the spring of 1943 the soaring inflation had leveled off.

National War Labor Board. A wartime board which had to approve all wage changes and had the power to arbitrate labor disputes.

Minorities

Blacks. Segregation in the military continued, and race riots erupted in some cities. The Fair Employment Practices Committee was set up by Roosevelt to enforce Executive Order 8802, prohibiting discrimination in plants with defense contracts. This order opened up better jobs for black workers.

Japanese. About 110,000 Americans of Japanese ancestry were sent to internment camps because of the fear that if the Japanese attacked the West Coast, they might be disloyal. *Korematsu* v. *U.S.* (1944) was a Supreme Court decision which upheld the right of the government to relocate AJA's in camps. A second Supreme Court decision, *Ex parte Endo,* forbade the internment of Japanese-American citizens who had been born in the United States.

War in Europe

Vichy government. The French puppet government established by the Nazis in the town of Vichy from 1940 to 1944. It was headed by the French World War I hero Marshal Henri-Philippe Pétain, and those who cooperated with the Nazi occupation were known as *collaborationists.* A Free French government-in-exile was organized in Great Britain by Charles De Gaulle, who considered himself the true leader of the French people.

June 6, 1944: D-Day. The day on which the Allied forces invaded France. The letter "D" stood for Day; the date was kept secret. The forces, gathered in England, were commanded by General Dwight Eisenhower. They stormed ashore at five points along the coast of Normandy, a province of France. The troops were supported by thousands of planes and paratroops, and after their success, victory was certain although another year of fighting remained. Note the map "World War II, European Theater" on p. 696.

1944–1945, Battle of the Bulge. The last great counterattack of the German army against the Allies. With this surprise attack, the Germans hoped to break through to the port of Antwerp, Belgium, thus splitting the Allied armies in two. Within several months, the line had been restored by Eisenhower's troops. Casualties were high and Eisenhower's final offensive was delayed, but the German's last reserves were destroyed.

General Dwight Eisenhower (1890–1969). Military leader who directed the North African invasion in 1943 and the Normandy landing in 1944, rising to the rank of five-star general. He became commander in chief of Supreme Headquarters, Allied Expeditionary Forces.

General George Patton (1885–1945). A West Point graduate who commanded troops in North Africa, was head of the United States Seventh Army as it swept through Sicily in 1943, and led the Third Army from the invasion of France in 1944 to the ends of the war. Patton was called "old blood and guts" and was known for his quick temper and outspoken comments.

May 8, 1945. Germany officially surrendered.

War in the Pacific

1942, Battle of the Coral Sea. The first naval engagement in which no surface vessels met in combat. It was fought entirely by carrier-based airplanes. Although superficially a Japanese victory because of the sinking of the United States carrier *Lexington,* the Japanese transports were forced to turn back and did not attack their destination, Port Moresby in New Guinea. See the map "World War II, Pacific Theater," on p. 699.

General Douglas MacArthur (1880–1964). A West Point graduate who commanded the defense of the Philippines, but when the islands were overrun by the Japanese in 1942, he left with a promise to return. He participated in the defense of Australia and in April 1942, was appointed commander of Allied forces in the Southwest Pacific. For two years MacArthur and his forces island-hopped from New Guinea toward the Philippines and finally returned to the latter in October 1944. As a five-star general, he received the Japanese surrender on September 2, 1945, and commanded the occupation forces of Japan from 1945 to 1951.

Admiral Chester Nimitz (1885–1966). Annapolis graduate who commanded the Pacific Fleet. His forces island-hopped through the Central Pacific until his ships and planes were within effective bombing distance of Japan.

Kamikaze pilots. Japanese suicide pilots who flew beyond the range in which they would have adequate fuel to return to Japan and crashed their bomb-laden planes against American warships and airstrips. See the photos on p. 701.

Hiroshima and Nagasaki. Two cities in Japan where atomic bombs were dropped on August 6 and August 9, 1945, respectively. President Truman made the decision based on past experience which indicated that the Japanese army might fight to the last man. Furthermore, he wanted to end the Pacific war before Russia could intervene effectively and thus claim a role in the peacemaking. The destruction of persons and buildings by the bombs was catastrophic, and on August 15, 1945, Japan surrendered.

Some Benefits from the War

Totalitarianism was dead in Germany, Italy, and Japan.

Cooperation with the Soviet Union during the war led many to hope for continued improved feelings.

Isolationism almost disappeared in the United States.

Technological advances and improvements in transportation and communication were made.

The power of the atom could, hopefully, be used for peaceful purposes.

Penicillin and other life-saving antibiotics were developed.

The United Nations was formed to promote international cooperation and preserve peace.

OTHER TERMS TO IDENTIFY

Walter Millis. Author of a best seller *The Road to War: America, 1914–1917* (1935). Millis' thesis was that certain factors had pulled the United States into World War I, such as British propaganda, heavy purchases of American supplies by the Allies, and Wilson's favoring the British when they violated neutral rights, as opposed to when the Germans committed violations. Such ideas became popular and generated support for the Neutrality Acts.

Phony war. The lull during the winter of 1939–1940 in which no real fighting took place. Great Britain and France declared war on Germany in September 1939, after Hitler invaded Poland. But it was not until April 1940, that the Germans moved once again, conquering Denmark, Norway, the Netherlands, Belgium, and France.

Rome-Berlin-Tokyo Axis. A mutual-assistance agreement signed by Italy, Germany, and Japan in 1940, promising total aid for a period of ten years. Italy and Germany had already established the Rome-Berlin Axis in 1936.

Committee to Defend America by Aiding the Allies. An interventionist organization headed by the Republican William Allen White, editor of the Emporia, Kansas *Gazette.* It was composed of members of both parties and rapidly gained strength in 1940.

America First Committee. A bipartisan isolationist organization led by Robert E. Wood of Sears Roebuck.

Four Freedoms. The idealistic goals for which the war was being fought, according to Roosevelt in 1941 as he persuaded the officially neutral United States to support Lend-Lease. They were freedom of speech, freedom of religion, freedom from want, and freedom from fear.

Smith-Connally War Labor Disputes Act. An act, passed over Roosevelt's veto, which gave the president the power to take over any plant making war materiel which was threatened by a strike. It also declared as illegal strikes against plants which had been seized.

Guadalcanal Island. Site of a battle in the Pacific from August 1942 to February 1943, in which the American forces finally drove out the Japanese.

Manhattan Project. Government-sponsored atomic research, officially established in May 1943. Development of materials for an atomic bomb took place at several sites, and the first successful bomb was exploded at Alamogordo, New Mexico, in July 1945. The project was considered a race with the Germans because it was known that German scientists had been conducting atomic research in the 1930s. Some of those scientists were Jews who later fled to America to escape Nazi anti-Semitism.

GLOSSARY

appeasement. The sacrifice of moral principle to avert aggression. At the 1938 Munich Conference, France and Great Britain appeased Hitler by agreeing to the Sudetenland's annexation by Germany.

Aryan. In Nazi ideology, a person of a supposedly superior Caucasian race with no Jewish background.

beachhead. A position on an enemy shoreline made by advance troops of an invading force. On D-Day, June 6, 1944, Allied forces established a solid beachhead along the Normandy coast, and within a few days 1 million Allied troops were on French soil.

Blitzkreig. A German term meaning "lightning war." It is a swift, sudden military offensive, usually by land and air forces. Between April 9 and June 22, 1939, the world saw *Blitzkrieg* in action as Nazi forces conquered Denmark, Norway, the Netherlands, Belgium, and France.

bridgehead. A military position established by advance troops on the enemy's side of a river to protect the main attacking force.

conscientious objector. One who on the basis of religious or moral principles refuses to bear arms or participate in military service. During World War II exemption from combat duty was usually granted to members of pacifist religious groups, such as the Society of Friends (Quakers) and Jehovah's Witnesses, who participated in noncombatant military service or some public service activity. Others were treated more harshly, however, and between 1940 and 1945 about 5,000 of the 100,000 conscientious objectors were imprisoned.

cryptanalyst. A person who analyzes or deciphers codes and other secret writings. An American cryptanalyst, Colonel William F. Friedman, had "cracked" the Japanese diplomatic code, and therefore the United States knew that war was imminent.

discretionary arms embargo. A refusal to sell military equipment to a country based on the judgment of a particular situation. As early as 1931 Secretary of State Stimson worked for a discretionary arms embargo law to be applied by the president in time of war against whichever side had broken the peace.

Albert Einstein (1879–1955). A German theoretical physicist who, because he was a Jew, left Nazi Germany in 1933 and moved to the United States to teach at Princeton. In 1939 Einstein sent a letter to President

Roosevelt regarding the potential of nuclear energy in warfare which influenced the Administration to set up the Manhattan Project.

Führer. The title of Adolf Hitler as the leader of the German Nazis. It is the German word for "leader" or "guide."

Hun. A member of a barbarian Asiatic tribe which invaded Europe around 450 A.D. Hun is also used to refer to a German.

indiscriminate bombing. Dropping bombs on any site, even civilian residential areas, rather than concentrating on military bases and munitions factories.

ostrichlike. The act of copying the ostrich's alleged habit of burying its head in the sand to escape disagreeable situations. In the early 1930s, the United States practiced ostrichlike isolationism.

override a veto. A method by which Congress can pass a law that the president does not like. For a bill to become a law, it must pass both the House and the Senate with a majority vote. Then the president either signs it and the bill becomes a law, or he vetoes it and sends it back to the chamber where it originated. If both houses pass it again, this time with a *two-thirds vote,* the bill becomes a law, overriding the presidential veto.

panzer division. A mechanized, armored military offensive unit. Panzer is the German word for "armor."

payroll-deduction system. A method of paying income taxes, proposed by Beardsley Ruml, chairman of the Federal Reserve Bank of New York, whereby employers "withheld" the taxes of wage earners and salaried personnel and paid them directly to the government. This system is still in use today.

"quarantine" speech. A 1937 speech by President Roosevelt in which he compared war to a disease which needed to be quarantined, that is, isolated. He proposed a "quarantine" of nations which were aggressors but was forced to abandon his idea by Americans who feared the result of such action.

Shylock. A heartless, exacting creditor. The term is after Shylock, the ruthless moneylender in Shakespeare's *Merchant of Venice* (1595). During the 1920s the European Allies resented repaying the war debts, and the French referred to the United States as *l'oncle Shylock.*

Spanish Civil War (1936–1939). In 1931 the king fled Spain, and a republican form of government was established. By 1936 the right-wing military, business, and religious leaders felt the government was becoming too liberal and started a revolt, led by General Francisco Franco. Republicans, also called loyalists or reds, received some aid from the Soviet Union, whereas Italy and Germany helped the victorious Franco and his Falangist party. Because of foreign involvement, the Spanish Civil War was sometimes called the dress rehearsal for World War II.

Spartans at Thermopylae. Spartans were inhabitants of Sparta, an area in Greece where civilization flourished from the 7th to the 4th centuries

B.C. Thermopylae was a mountainous pass in eastern Greece which was the site of an heroic but unsuccessful defense by the Spartans against the invading Persians in 480 B.C. The Japanese fought like the Spartans at Thermopylae to hold on to the Pacific islands they had occupied.

Third Reich. A term referring to the German government under the Nazis from 1933 to 1945. The First Reich was the Holy Roman Empire (800s–1806), and the Second Reich was the German Empire (1871–1919).

OFFICERS IN THE MILITARY

ARMY AND AIR FORCE	NAVY
General of the Army (5 stars)	Fleet Admiral
General	Admiral
Lieutenant General	Vice Admiral
Major General	Rear Admiral
Brigadier General	Commodore (wartime only)
Colonel	Captain
Lieutenant Colonel	Commander
Major	Lieutenant Commander
Captain	Lieutenant
First Lieutenant	Lieutenant (junior grade)
Second Lieutenant	Ensign

WORDS TO KNOW

Define the following, using the dictionary if necessary.

abeyance	euphemistically
colloquialism	ferreting
cryptic	hamstrung
disingenuously	octogenarian
egocentric	poseur

SAMPLE QUESTIONS

Multiple Choice

1. Not a part of isolationism in the 1920s and 1930s was:
   a. tariffs.
   b. Lend-Lease.
   c. Neutrality Acts.
   d. immigration quotas.
2. The Stimson Doctrine for Manchuria:
   a. was a protest against Japan's policy.

   b. prevented Japan's projected seizure.
   c. criticized Chiang Kai-shek.
   d. became part of the Kellogg-Briand Pact.
3. The Nye Committee's findings indicated that:
   a. the United States was wrong to enter Japan.
   b. the pay of congressmen should be doubled.
   c. DuPont and other munitions manufacturers pulled the United States into World War I.
   d. the Good Neighbor policy was a failure.
4. Limitations on civil liberty during World War II included the:
   a. removal of Japanese-Americans from the West Coast.
   b. imprisonment of many communists.
   c. internment of most Italian-Americans.
   d. close censorship of all mail within the United States.
5. In the conduct of World War II the United States adhered to *all but one* of the following policies:
   a. victory in Europe first.
   b. unconditional surrender.
   c. recognition of the Free French rather than the Vichy government.
   d. all Axis powers surrender at the same time.

True-False

1. The Kellogg-Briand Pact (1928) declared that war was no longer an instrument of foreign policy.
2. The European allies of World War I paid their war debts in full.
3. The policy of appeasement toward Hitler was set forth in the Good Neighbor policy.
4. President Roosevelt knew exactly when the Japanese were going to strike Pearl Harbor but failed to tell Secretary of State Hull.
5. General MacArthur and Admiral Nimitz were military leaders against the Japanese in the Pacific.

ANSWERS
Multiple Choice: b, a, c, a, d. True-False: T, F, F, F, T.

28

Foreign Affairs
1942-1964

CHRONOLOGY

1945	Yalta Conference
1945	Potsdam Conference
1945	United Nations founded
1947	Truman Doctrine
1947	Marshall Doctrine
1948	Berlin Airlift
1949	NATO founded
1950–1953	Korean conflict
1957	Eisenhower Doctrine
1960	U-2 affair
1961	Bay of Pigs invasion
1962	Cuban missile crisis

CHAPTER CHECKLIST

Wartime Conferences

1943, Teheran Conference. The first Big Three conference of World War II in which Franklin Roosevelt, Winston Churchill, and Joseph Stalin met to discuss war strategy. At this meeting in Iran, Stalin reaffirmed an earlier promise to bring Russia into the war against Japan as soon as Germany surrendered. He also agreed on the need for an international organization to replace the now defunct League of Nations.

1945, Yalta Conference. The last meeting of Roosevelt, Churchill, and Stalin. At this conference, held in the USSR, Roosevelt agreed to restore territory to Russia which she had lost in the 1905 Russo-Japanese War. The most critical question concerned establishing governments in the countries of eastern Europe as they were liberated from Nazi control, primarily by Russian armies. Poland was discussed, and Stalin agreed to allow free elections in the reconstituted Polish republic. This was never done, and a pro-Russian puppet regime was established. Similar situations developed in the other eastern European countries as Russia created a buffer zone of communist "satellite" countries everywhere that Russian armies moved in.

1945, Potsdam Conference. A July meeting held in Potsdam, a suburb of Berlin, attended by Truman, Stalin, and Churchill, who was replaced by a new prime minister, Clement Attlee, during the conference. At Potsdam, the Big Three agreed to try the Nazi leaders as war criminals and confirmed the division of Germany into four zones, to be occupied separately by American, Russian, British, and French forces. The city of Berlin, which was in the Russian sector, was also divided into zones. Other postwar problems could not be successfully negotiated as both Truman and Stalin began to harden their stances.

United Nations

1944, Dumbarton Oaks Conference. The representatives of the United States, the Soviet Union, Great Britain, and China met at Dumbarton Oaks, an estate outside Washington, D.C. They drafted proposals for an international organization which formed the basis of the United Nations charter.

1945, San Francisco Conference. A meeting of 50 nations from April to June which debated, drafted, and signed the United Nations charter.

United Nations. An international organization with headquarters in New York City. Every member has a seat in the General Assembly, but the 11-member Security Council is the real decision-making body. Five of the 11 are permanent members and have veto power: the United States, Great Britain, France, Russia, and China—the major allies of World War II. Originally China was represented by the nationalist Chinese government of Chiang Kai-shek, which has been located on the island of Taiwan since 1949. However, in 1971 the nationalist Chinese were replaced by representatives of the communist People's Republic of China.

The routine administration of the United Nations is handled by the *Secretariat,* headed by a secretary general. Other divisions provided for in the charter are the Trusteeship Council and the International Court of Justice. The Economic and Social Council oversees a number of related agencies such as the International Monetary Fund, the World Health Organization, and the United Nations Educational, Scientific, and Cultural Organization (UNESCO).

Containment Policy

Containment. The foreign policy adopted by the United States after World War II to restrain the spread of communism and confine it to its boundaries at that time. The key ideas were those of a Foreign Service officer, George Kennan, who in an anonymous article in *Foreign Affairs* (July 1947), stated that "firm and vigilant containment" based on the "application of counter-force" was the best means of dealing with Soviet pressures. He also proposed that a broad aid program be offered to countries.

1947, Truman Doctrine. Truman declared that the United States would resist communist expansion, particularly in Greece and Turkey. The governments of these two countries were threatened by communist guerrilla groups, and Great Britain, which had been aiding these governments, announced that she could no longer afford to do so. Therefore, Truman went before Congress and asked for $400 million in military and economic aid for Greece and Turkey. He declared that there was a struggle between "two ways of life" and that the United States should "help free people to maintain their free institutions . . . against aggressive movements that seek to impose upon them totalitarian regimes." The Truman Doctrine achieved its purpose; that is, Greece and Turkey did not become communist.

1947, Marshall Plan. A proposal made by Secretary of State George C. Marshall to promote the economic recovery of Europe and thus lessen the popularity of the growing communist parties in those countries. Marshall invited the European nations to draw up a joint plan, and the United States would provide economic assistance. The offer was also open to the Soviet Union and its satellite nations, but they refused. Between 1948 and 1952 the United States provided about $14 billion, and the effort was highly successful. Not only did Europe surpass its prewar economic production, but initial steps were taken toward greater economic unity in Europe, leading to the Common Market.

1948, Berlin Airlift. A measure designed to keep Berlin, Germany, from being completely absorbed by the surrounding Russian-occupied East Germany. In this conflict, the communists blockaded all road and rail routes between Berlin and West Germany. Instead of abandoning Berlin, Truman decided to have United States planes fly supplies, including food and fuel, to the city, and after 11 months, the Soviets lifted their blockade. Thereafter two permanent German governments were established: the Federal Republic of Germany (West Germany) and the German Democratic Republic (communist East Germany).

1949, North Atlantic Treaty Organization. An alliance formed to deter possible aggression by the Soviet Union and provide a military arm for the policy of containment. In the treaty, the nations agreed "that an armed attack against one or more of them in Europe or North America shall be considered an attack against them all." NATO headquarters were located in Paris, France, until 1967, and then at France's request were moved to a site near Brussels, Belgium.

Containment Policy in Asia

Japan. After V-J Day (August 15, 1945) Truman was determined that Russia, which had finally declared war on Japan on August 8, 1945, would not move in and set up communist puppet governments as she had in eastern Europe. Consequently, an Allied Control Council was established, but American troops, commanded by General MacArthur, ran the country. In 1951 a peace treaty formally ended the occupation, and Japan emerged firmly allied with the United States.

China. Conflict between the government of Chiang Kai-shek and a communist guerrilla movement led by Mao Tse-tung had existed since the 1930s, and as soon as the war ended, the United States tried to install Chiang in control of all China. Truman sent General George Marshall to arrange a settlement between Chiang and Mao in 1946, but neither would make significant concessions. Between 1947 and 1949 full-scale civil war raged. By 1949 Mao's communists controlled China, and Chiang's nationalists had fled to the island of Formosa, now called Taiwan. The United States continued to recognize Chiang's government as the official one of China.

Korea. After the war Korea was taken from Japan and divided along the 38th parallel, the Russian controlling the northern half, the Americans the southern. Both agreed to a unified and independent republic at some future date, but by 1948 two "independent" governments had been set up, and the Americans withdrew their troops. In 1950, however, communist North Korea sent armored divisions south of the 38th parallel where they were quickly victorious over the weak South Korean forces. The United States, with the backing of the United Nations' Security Council, sent in planes and ground troops. *General Douglas MacArthur* was placed in command, and 16 nations supplied troops for the United Nations forces, although 90 percent were Americans. MacArthur wanted to bomb and blockade Communist China, which was helping North Korea, but Truman, fearing a third world war, refused. The general then made public statements criticizing administration policies, and Truman finally removed him from command. In 1953 a treaty was negotiated, and Korea remained divided. The United States had suffered over 135,000 casualties, including 33,000 dead. The policy of containment had been successful but expensive.

Communism at Home

Hiss-Chambers case. In 1948 *Whittaker Chambers,* a former communist and an editor of *Time,* testified before the House Un-American Activities Committee that ten years earlier *Alger Hiss* had given him secret State Department documents to relay to the Russians. Hiss had been a State Department official until 1947 when he became president of the Carnegie

Endowment for International Peace. When Chambers repeated the charge on television, Hiss sued him for libel. Chambers then produced the incriminating microfilms, and the government charged Hiss with perjury, that is, falsely testifying. He could not be indicted for espionage because the statute of limitations, in this instance five years, had run out. There was a deadlock in the first trial in 1949, but in the second Hiss was convicted and sentenced to five years in prison. The case was important because it reflected the fear of communist influence on American policy.

Joseph McCarthy (1909–1957). Republican senator from Wisconsin who made wild charges between 1950 and 1954 concerning alleged American communists. His first accusations were made in a speech before the Women's Republican Club of Wheeling, West Virginia, in which he claimed that the State Department was infested with "card-carrying communists." He continued to point out famous people who were probable communists, using guilt-by-association tactics. McCarthyism came to mean public accusations of disloyalty or subversion with little regard to evidence. Finally in 1954 McCarthy was officially censured by the Senate.

Foreign Policy Under Eisenhower

John Foster Dulles (1888–1959). Secretary of state from 1953 to 1959 who formulated a new policy for fighting the communists in the Cold War. Instead of simply "containing" communism, Dulles felt the United States should warn Russia and China that if they actively supported communist guerrilla movements in other countries, the United States would not send troops to fight a brushfire war as they had in Korea. Instead, the United States threatened *massive retaliation,* that is, it would aim its missiles directly toward Moscow or Peking. This policy was sometimes referred to as brinkmanship, for it would conceivably push the country to the brink of war. Dulles' policy was more idealistic and more aggressive than Truman's policy of containment, but it was not successful for the United States was unprepared to carry through these threats. At the same time, Russian policy began to shift as Nikita Khrushchev talked of "peaceful coexistence" between communism and capitalism.

Vietnam. An area which was a French colony from the 19th century, was dominated by the Japanese in conjunction with the Vichy government during World War II, and was reclaimed by the French after the war. However, a group within the country wanted independence, and these *Vietminh* were led by the communist Ho Chi Minh and aided by Communist China. In keeping with the policy of containment, Truman sent economic and military assistance to the French. This practice was continued by Eisenhower. But in 1954 the Vietminh trapped the French army at *Dien Bien Phu,* and when the French requested United States Air Force assistance and were refused, the French garrison finally surrendered.

1954, Geneva agreement. France, Great Britain, Russia, and China met in Switzerland to determine the future of Vietnam. The French withdrew, and the country was divided along the 17th parallel. The communist Ho Chi Minh controlled the northern sector, called the Democratic Republic of Vietnam, while the southern part remained prowestern and received United States aid.

1956, Suez crisis. In an attempt to improve relations with Egypt, the United States offered to help finance the Aswan Dam, which would facilitate an important irrigation project on the Nile. Meanwhile, however, *Gamal Abdel Nasser* of Egypt negotiated a treaty with Russia in which he exchanged Egyptian cotton for armaments. Realizing that economic assistance was not making Nasser pro-American, Dulles withdrew the Aswan Dam offer, and Nasser retaliated by nationalizing the Suez Canal, purportedly to obtain money for the Nile irrigation project. Shortly thereafter Israel attacked Egypt, and Great Britain and France took advantage of the situation to reoccupy Port Said at the northern end of the canal. The United States and the United Nations denounced the intervention, and a ceasefire was quickly arranged. But American allies were disenchanted with Dulles' actions in trying to win Arab friendship without abandoning Israel, and Russia moved into the power vacuum and helped build the dam.

1957, Eisenhower Doctrine. A resolution passed by Congress, at the request of President Eisenhower, which in effect applied the policy of containment to the Middle East. It gave the president the authority to send armed forces to any nation "requesting assistance against armed aggression from any country controlled by international communism."

1960, U-2 affair. An American U-2 reconnaissance plane was shot down over Russia by antiaircraft fire. At first United States officials said it was a weather plane which had strayed off course. When the Russians later announced that the pilot, Francis Gary Powers, was alive and had confessed he was a spy, it was obvious that the United States had lied. The event was particularly significant because a summit conference in Paris had already been planned. Khrushchev arrived raging; Eisenhower refused to apologize; and the committee meeting collapsed. Powers was returned to the United States in exchange for a Russian spy in 1962.

Cuba. In 1959 a revolutionary movement led by *Fidel Castro* overthrew the dictatorship of Fulgencio Batista, and President Eisenhower quickly recognized Castro's government. But Castro's anti-Americanism soon became obvious as he set up a communist government and established close relations with the Soviet Union.

1961, Bay of Pigs invasion. Anti-Castro Cuban exiles staged an invasion of the island with the assistance of American guns and ships. They had been trained in Central America by members of the Central Intelligence Agency. Kennedy refused to send air support when it was requested at the last minute, and the invasion failed. The United States' involvement could not be disguised and left the country open to criticism for intervening in Latin American affairs.

1962, Cuban missile crisis. Russia built guided missile sites in Cuba with the capacity to deliver hydrogen warheads to both North and South America. When these were discovered, President Kennedy ordered a blockade of Cuba to prevent a further buildup. He also told Khrushchev to dismantle the missile bases and remove all weapons capable of striking the United States. Khrushchev finally agreed, and Kennedy lifted the blockade. This action enhanced the United States diplomatic prestige and lessened Sovet-American tensions.

OTHER TERMS TO IDENTIFY

Joseph E. Davies (1876–1958). Ambassador to the Soviet Union (1937–1938) who wrote a best-selling book, *Mission to Moscow* (1941), in which he praised the Russian people and their communist leaders, particularly Joseph Stalin.

1941, Atlantic Charter. A joint declaration issued by President Roosevelt and Prime Minister Churchill on the U.S.S. *Augusta* off the coast of Newfoundland in August 1941. The United States was still officially neutral, but Great Britain and the United States declared their intentions not to annex any territory, affirmed the right of self-government, and adhered to such principles as freedom from want and fear. This statement of principles had sometimes been compared with Wilson's Fourteen Points during World War I.

1942, Declaration of the United Nations. A statement signed by 26 nations expressing their willingness to cooperate in solving postwar problems. The Allies agreed not to annex territory, to respect the right of people to select their own form of government, to promote economic cooperation, and to force the disarmament of the aggressor nations of Germany, Italy, and Japan.

Southeast Asia Treaty Organization (SEATO). An alliance formed in 1954 which was Dulles' response to the French defeat in Vietnam. Nations which signed the pact included the United States, Great Britain, France, Australia, New Zealand, but only three Asian nations: the Philippine Republic, Thailand, and Pakistan.

1955, Geneva summit conference. A meeting in Switzerland of President Eisenhower, Prime Minister Anthony Eden of Great Britain, French Premier Edgar Faure, and Nikita Khrushchev and Nikolai Bulganin of the Soviet Union to discuss disarmament and the reunification of West and East Germany. No real agreements were reached, but some observers noticed a lessening of Cold War tensions and called the new atmosphere "the spirit of Geneva."

Organization of American States (OAS). A regional agency within the United Nations chartered in 1948. The headquarters is at the Pan American Union in Washington, D.C., but the United States has neither a veto nor any special position in this hemispheric organization.

Alliance for Progress. A proposal made by President Kennedy to strengthen Latin American countries economically so that they would not be attracted to communism as Cuba had been. The alliance was signed by 20 American republics, and the United States spent billions on such projects as low-cost housing, education, and pleas for population control.

Peace Corps. A volunteer organization created by President Kennedy in 1962 to provide person-to-person technical assistance to developing countries. Peace Corps volunteers serve outside the United States for two-year periods.

1963, Test-Ban Treaty. An agreement of the major powers, except France and China, banning the testing of nuclear weapons in the atmosphere. The treaty was a small but significant step toward disarmament.

GLOSSARY

Central Intelligence Agency (CIA). An undercover organization which coordinates intelligence operations for all governmental agencies. It was created in 1947 and is under the authority of the National Security Council.

Central Treaty Organization (CENTO). A Middle East alliance formed in 1959 by Turkey, Iran, Pakistan, and Great Britain. Although the United States has bilateral agreements of cooperation with these nations, it is not part of the alliance.

Sir Winston Churchill (1874–1965). British statesman and historian who was prime minister of Great Britain from 1940 to 1945 and again from 1951 to 1955.

Cold War. The state of rivalry between the Soviet Union and the United States and their respective allies following World War II.

Colossus. A huge statue, 120 feet high, of the Greek god Apollo, built about 280 B.C. It was set at the entrance to the harbor of ancient Rhodes, an island in the Aegean Sea which is now part of Greece. At the close of World War II, the United States stood, as Cassius said of Caesar, "bestride the narrow world like a Colossus."

Cyrillic alphabet. An old Slavic alphabet supposedly invented by Saint Cyril (827–869), a Christian missionary. It is presently used in modified form for Russian and other Slavic languages. At Yalta Stalin gave Roosevelt a photograph of himself with a long Cyrillic inscription.

French Indochina. The former French colonies and protectorates of Cochin China, Annam, and Tonkin, which are now Vietnam, Laos, and Cambodia. These areas became independent of France in 1954.

hot line. A telephone from the White House in Washington, D.C., to the

Kremlin, which houses the offices of the Soviet government in Moscow, so that the two nations can be in instant communication in a crisis. It was installed after the 1962 Cuban missile crisis.

hung jury. A jury which is unable to come to a decision. In many criminal cases the decision must be unanimous, but in some cases a verdict can be rendered even if some of the jury disagree, as in a nine to three decision.

Iron Curtain. The political and ideological barrier between the Soviet bloc and western Europe after World War II. The term was first used by Winston Churchill in a speech at Westminster College in Missouri on March 5, 1946. He said it was as if an iron curtain had descended on eastern Europe, behind which Russian control was increasing.

Nikita Khrushchev (1894–1971). The foremost political figure in the USSR from around 1955 until 1964 when he was forced to retire. As first secretary of the Soviet Communist party's Central Committee from 1953, he was head of the party, and as chairman of the Council of Ministers from 1958, he was head of the government.

libel. A written or pictorial statement that damages a person by defaming his character or exposing him to ridicule. Alger Hiss denied the charge that he had been a communist in the 1930s and sued Whittaker Chambers for libel.

Middle East. The area in Asia and Africa between and including Libya in the west, Pakistan in the east, Turkey in the north, and the Arabian Peninsula in the south.

"revisionist" historians. Scholars of history who present a new or corrected version of an event.

Pekingese. Small dog of a breed developed in China. "Unleashing" Chiang Kai-shek against mainland Communist China would have been like matching a Pekingese against a tiger.

perjury. The deliberate giving of a false testimony by a witness under oath in a criminal proceeding. Alger Hiss was convicted of perjury in 1950.

saber rattling. A very open display of military power or the threatening of war.

soviet. A council in the Union of Soviet Socialist Republics (USSR). A soviet is the supreme local authority and consists of representatives of workmen, soldiers, and peasants. It sends deputies to a soviet congress or higher body which has authority over a larger area. The highest governmental body is the Supreme Soviet.

Sputnik. The artificial earth satellite launched by the USSR, that is, Russia, on October 4, 1957. The United States did not launch an earth satellite until January 1958, and Americans fell behind in the space race.

Joseph Stalin (1879–1953). The undisputed leader of the Soviet Union from 1929 until 1953.

statute of limitations. A law setting a time limit on the enforcement of an act. In 1949 Alger Hiss could not be charged with espionage committed in the 1930s because the statute of limitations, in this case five years, had run out. The statute of limitations varies according to the crime.

Suez Canal. A 107 miles long waterway in Egypt, which connects the Mediterranean Sea and the Gulf of Suez, and thence the Red Sea. It was constructed from 1859 to 1869 by Ferdinand de Lesseps, who later made an unsuccessful attempt to build a canal across the isthmus of Panama. The British held the controlling interest in the canal from 1875 to 1956.

WORDS TO KNOW

Define the following, using the dictionary if necessary.

contretemps	perfervid
efficacious	presaging
lexicon	sanctimonious
mastiff	supinely
pathological	ubiquitous

SAMPLE QUESTIONS

Multiple Choice

1. Who of the following foreshadowed the policy of containment in an article in *Foreign Affairs?*
   a. Dean Acheson.
   b. George Marshall.
   c. George Kennan.
   d. Winston Churchill.
2. The Marshall Plan provided for:
   a. a coalition government in China.
   b. the organization of NATO.
   c. massive economic assistance for Europe.
   d. the Berlin airlift.
3. One associates the doctrine of "massive retaliation" with which of the following foreign affairs leaders?
   a. Dean Acheson.
   b. Adlai Stevenson.
   c. John Foster Dulles.
   d. John Fitzgerald Kennedy.
4. "I have here in my hand . . . a list of names that were known to the secretary of state as being members of the Communist party and who nevertheless are still working and shaping . . . policy." These are the words of:

    a. John Foster Dulles.
    b. Franklin Roosevelt.
    c. Eugene McCarthy.
    d. Joseph McCarthy.
5. All of the following occurred while John Kennedy was president *except:*
    a. the censure of Senator Joseph McCarthy.
    b. the formation of the Alliance for Progress.
    c. the Bay of Pigs invasion.
    d. the Cuban missile crisis.

True-False

1. At the Potsdam Conference (1945) the Big Three confirmed the division of postwar Germany into four zones.
2. Each of the five permanent members of the UN Security Council has the veto power.
3. The Eisenhower Doctrine provided for military and economic aid to Greece and Turkey.
4. The North Atlantic Treaty Organization was established in reaction to the U-2 affair.
5. General MacArthur was removed from Korea for publicly criticizing President Truman's policies.

Portfolio Six
The Painter's Eye

PORTFOLIO CHECKLIST

"Ashcan" school. Originally known as "The Eight," these artists depicted their surroundings as they saw them rather than simply paint "proper" subjects. Their works were first viewed by a shocked public in 1908 at a special exhibit they arranged. Robert Henri was the teacher and leader of the "ashcan" school.

Pioneers of modernism. American painters flocked to Paris and copied the art movements flourishing there. The first American modernist style was synchromism, which was comprised of planes of color and was nonrepresentational; that is, it did not include recognizable figures.

Precisionists. A loosely knit group of painters who used modern technology as subject matter: bridges, skyscrapers, and even kitchen gadgets.

Regionalists. Artists who disliked the influence of Europe's modern trends and instead wanted to portray what they saw as American reality. The rural regionalists visually expressed the virtues of America's farmlands and small towns. The urban regionalists were primarily in New York City and painted the multifaceted life of that metropolis.

Social realists. Artists whose works reflected an awareness of and concern for social problems in America. Their paintings were designed to appeal to emotions as they portrayed some of the injustices of society.

Public support of the arts. During the lean years of the Depression, the federal government came to the aid of artists through several programs, including the Federal Art Project. The project lasted from 1935 to 1943 and financed thousands of paintings and sculptures in a variety of styles. In 1966 the National Endowment for the Arts was created, and other governmental and corporate bodies have commissioned, collected, and otherwise encouraged the arts. Such sponsorship has not contributed to censorship as it has in the Soviet Union.

Abstract expressionists. Artists who avoided painting objects and instead emphasized spontaneous expressions with color. The movement's chief theoretician was Hans Hofmann, who explained that art should reflect the painter's subconscious rather than the outside world. These artists of the 1940s and 1950s were commonly called the New York School, because their works were usually sold in galleries in that city. New York replaced Paris as the art capital of the world.

Experiments in perception and design. Art of the 1960s became more diverse and was often detached and scientific in its approach. The minimalists painted huge canvases which seemed monochromatic, that is, one colored, but closer inspection revealed a slight variation of shade. Other artists abandoned the traditional rectangular frame for "shaped canvas" in other geometric shapes. Op artists created visual, or optical, illusions through color and design.

Pop art. Artists of the popular and commercial image who satirized contemporary America. Their art in the 1960s was a countermovement to the highly abstract work of the previous two decades. Some painted comic-strip cartoons; others painted visual takeoffs of famous personalities, all reflecting our mass culture.

Realism. Whatever the trend of the moment, representational art, that is, easily recognizable figures, continued to endure. The new realism of the 1970s was a photorealist record of Americans and their culture, often a harsh portrayal of the blemishes.

OTHER TERMS TO IDENTIFY

Armory Show. An international art exhibit sponsored by the Association of American Painters and Sculptors and held in New York's 69th Regiment Armory. For the first time modern works by European and American artists were extensively shown side by side.

Thomas Hart Benton (1889–1975). A regionalist painter who was named after his famous uncle, Thomas Hart Benton (1782–1858), senator from Missouri. The artist Benton found his subject matter in common American life and deplored the modern art movement.

Jackson Pollock (1912–1956). An abstract expressionist who painted by dripping or splattering paint and building up dense, glittering webs of color. His "action painting" reflected a new mood of freedom.

GLOSSARY

avant garde. In any field, the most daring and experimental innovations.

cubism. A school of painting and sculpture which developed in Paris in the early 20th century. Images were dissected and reassembled in new abstract forms, often as transparent, intersecting cubes or other geometric shapes.

calligraphy. The art of very fine and often ornate handwriting.

salad days. A term referring to the time of youth and inexperience, based on a Shakespearean quote, "my salad days when I was green in judgment, cold in blood." Many famous abstract expressionists of the 1950s received WPA funds in their salad days.

surrealism. A 20th-century movement in art and literature influenced by the theories of Sigmund Freud. Surrealist painters tried to express subconscious mental activities by presenting images without order or sequence, as in a dream.

WORDS TO KNOW

Define the following, using the dictionary if necessary.

amalgam	elegy
amorphous	moribund
Cyclopean	renascence
doyenne	seminal

29

The Postwar Scene 1945-1964

CHRONOLOGY

1947 Taft-Hartley Act
1954 *Brown* v. *Board of Education of Topeka*
1955 AFL-CIO merger
1963 Assassination of John Kennedy
1964 Civil Rights Act

CHAPTER CHECKLIST

Presidential Styles

Harry Truman. A Democratic president who felt unqualified to follow in Roosevelt's footsteps, yet wanted to make his own mark in history. He was not too successful in converting to a peacetime economy, and inflation angered both labor and business. Nor did his program of reform, called the *Fair Deal,* receive support in Congress, where he had alienated southern conservatives and northern liberals. Truman was a frank, down-to-earth individual who often got into controversies with politicians and reporters. Yet, in the final analysis, he was considered a strong executive and was reelected in his own right in a surprise victory over Thomas Dewey in 1948.

Dwight Eisenhower. A former military leader who tried to remain "above politics" as a Republican president. He concentrated on broad questions of policy and left details to subordinates. His chief assistant was Sherman Adams, former governor of New Hampshire, and many of his appointments were wealthy businessmen. His view of government was that it should be decentralized and that private enterprise, that is, the business community, should assume as much responsibility for the national welfare as possible. "Ike" was not a forceful president, but he was an extremely popular and trusted personality.

John Kennedy. A young, dynamic Democratic politician who appealed to the idealism of Americans. He read avidly and encouraged the arts by inviting leading scientists, writers, and musicians to the White House. However, he was not successful in getting his program, labeled the *New Frontier,* through Congress. Some felt that he was too reasonable and conciliatory. Whether this approach would eventually have paid off is not known because he was assassinated on November 22, 1963, in Dallas.

Lyndon Johnson. A forceful Democratic legislator who served in Congress for 23 years and was most effective as Senate majority leader. He was a master at persuading congressmen to vote for his proposals, which he hoped would create the *Great Society* in the United States. Johnson was a strong president who was reelected in his own right in 1964. But he became increasingly unpopular because of his escalation of the Vietnam War and decided not to seek another term in the interest of national unity.

Other National Leaders

Robert Alphonso Taft (1889–1953). Son of President Taft who made a name for himself as Republican senator from Ohio from 1939 to 1953. In foreign policy, Taft was an isolationist, and his conservatism in domestic affairs could be seen in his sponsoring of the Taft-Hartley Labor Management Act (1947). He was called "Mr. Republican" by his fellow party members.

Adlai Ewing Stevenson (1900–1965). An attorney, elected governor of Illinois in 1948, who was the unsuccessful Democratic presidential candidate against Eisenhower in 1952 and 1956. Stevenson was known as an intellectual with a sharp wit, traits which did not necessarily endear him or make him understandable to the common voter.

Richard Milhouse Nixon (1913–   ). A California Republican congressman who first became well known as a result of his investigation of the ex-communist, Alger Hiss, for the House Committee on Un-American Activities. He briefly served as senator and then became vice-president under President Eisenhower. In 1960 he lost the presidential race by a paper-thin margin to Kennedy, and in 1962 he lost the California gubernatorial race after which he blamed the press for his defeat. Nixon temporarily retired from public life and joined a New York law firm, but made a comeback in 1968 when he was elected president.

Joseph Raymond McCarthy (1909–1957). Republican senator from Wisconsin from 1947 to 1957 who became famous for his speeches accusing people of being communists. In 1953, after his appointment as chairman of the Permanent Subcommittee on Investigations, he began probing communism in the Army. The Army-McCarthy Hearings were televised nationwide in 1954, and McCarthy's actions were discredited. He was officially censured by the Senate in December of 1954.

HARRY S TRUMAN (1884–1972), 33rd President

Born in Missouri and entered politics as a Democrat after World
    War I.
Elected as a county judge in 1922.
United States senator (1934–1945).
Vice-president under Franklin Roosevelt (1945).
President (1945–1953).

DWIGHT DAVID EISENHOWER (1890–1969), 34th President

Born in Texas; grew up in Kansas; and graduated from West Point.
Commander in chief of Allied forces in Europe during World War II.
President of Columbia University in New York (1948–1950).
Commander of Supreme Headquarters, Allied Powers in Europe
    (SHAPE), which coordinates military forces for the North Atlantic
    Treaty Organization (NATO) (1950–1952).
President (1953–1961).

JOHN FITZGERALD KENNEDY (1917–1963), 35th President

Born in Massachusetts and graduated from Harvard.
Democratic member of the House of Representatives (1947–1953).
United States senator (1953–1961).
President (1961–1963).
Assassinated in Dallas, Texas, by Lee Harvey Oswald.

LYNDON BAINES JOHNSON (1908–1973), 36th President

Born in Texas and graduated from Southwest Texas State Teachers
    College in San Marcos.
Democratic member of the House of Representatives (1937–1949).
United States senator (1949–1961).
Vice-president under John Kennedy (1961–1963).
President (1963–1969).

Economy

1944, GI Bill of Rights. An act which provided veterans with loans to start new businesses. It also granted subsidies for veterans to continue their education and was responsible for the college boom after World War II.

Americans for Democratic Action. A group of former New Dealers who were disturbed by Truman's handling of economic and Cold War problems organized in 1947 to promote their middle-of-the-road economic and political ideas. They felt growth was essential and that the way to curb inflation was not through wage and price controls but through expanded production. Government and private enterprise should work together to achieve a "National Prosperity Budget." This economic strategy was not particularly effective during Truman's administration.

Labor

1947, Taft-Hartley Act. An act bitterly opposed by labor and passed over the veto of President Truman. It outlawed closed shops, secondary boycotts, jurisdictional disputes between unions, and union contributions to political campaigns. The act also compelled unions to register and file financial reports with the secretary of labor. Most important, in case of a strike which endangered national interests, it gave the president the right to issue an injunction forcing the workers to go back to work for an 80-day "cooling off" period. The Taft-Hartley Act reflected the antilabor sentiment aroused by the postwar strikes.

American Federation of Labor-Congress of Industrial Organizations (AFL-CIO). A formal merger of these two labor organizations took place in 1955. George Meany of the plumbers' union became its president. The AFL was founded in 1886 to organize skilled workers along craft lines, whereas the CIO, which became its rival in 1938, organized unskilled workers in such industries as steel and automobile. The merger indicated their recognition that both craft and industrial unions were needed, and it strengthened labor's influence.

1959, Landrum-Griffin Act. A measure, also known as the Labor-Management Reporting and Disclosure Act, designed to make labor leaders responsive to union members. It required union officials to be elected by secret ballot and union funds to be strictly controlled rather than invested and spent at the whim of the officials.

The Farm

Price-support system. A method used by the government to keep agricultural prices from falling too low and thus ruining the farmer. The system attempted to keep the prices of crops such as wheat and cotton near "parity" with the prices paid by farmers for manufactured goods. *Parity* is the level of farm product prices maintained by government support and intended to give farmers the same standard of living they enjoyed in a certain period. During the New Deal this system had been worked out using the years 1909–1914 as the basis for parity. There were several methods of achieving this standard:

Acreage controls. A system limiting the number of acres which a farmer could plant with a particular crop. This method would lower the supply of a product and thus hopefully raise the price. However, many farmers simply poured more fertilizer on their remaining acres and continued to increase output.

Government grain elevators and warehouses. Facilities used by the government to store nonperishable surplus crops. These crops were either purchased by the government and redistributed, or they were simply stored by the government until the price went up and the farmer could make a better profit. The storehouses did not help farmers who raised perishable commodities such as fruits and vegetables.

Soil bank. A program initiated in 1956 under which farmers were paid not to plant. Instead, some of their land was used for conservation purposes, usually planted with a crop which was then plowed under in order to revitalize the soil. By 1960 some 28.7 million acres had been placed in the soil bank.

Anticommunism

1940, Smith Act. A congressional act which made it illegal to advocate or teach the overthrow of the government by force or to be a member of an organization with these goals. The act was aimed at the Communist party, but during World War II, while the Soviets were allies, the law was not enforced. During the Truman era, however, it was used to jail the leaders of the American Communist party.

1951, *Dennis et al.* v. *U.S.* A Supreme Court decision which upheld the constitutionality of the Smith Act by convicting 11 leaders of the American Communist party.

1957, *Yates* v. *U.S.* A Supreme Court ruling which modified the Dennis case by holding that merely advocating revolution was not a crime.

1950, McCarran Internal Security Act. An act, passed over Truman's veto, designed to curb communist subversion. The law made it unlawful to perform any deed which might lead to the establishment of a totalitarian dictatorship. Communist-front organizations, that is, groups with innocent-sounding names whose leadership was communist, were required to register with the attorney general, and their members were barred from defense work. Furthermore, these people could not get a passport to travel abroad, nor were aliens who had ever belonged to a totalitarian organization admitted into the United States. Truman and others felt that this act violated the civil rights of individuals. In 1964 the

Supreme Court threw out the bar on passports, and in 1965 it disallowed an order requiring Communist party leaders to register.

The Black

1954, *Brown* v. *Board of Education of Topeka*. A Supreme Court decision which ruled that segregation in public schools was illegal. It reversed the "separate but equal" doctrine in *Plessy* v. *Ferguson* (1896) as Chief Justice Earl Warren declared, "Separate educational facilities are inherently unequal." Integration, however, proceeded slowly.

1957, Integration of Little Rock Central High School. In compliance with the Brown decision, the Little Rock, Arkansas, school board selected nine black students to integrate Central High School. Governor Orval M. Faubus tried to block the black students from attending by calling out the National Guard to stop them. Although President Eisenhower was not convinced of the wisdom of the Brown ruling, he felt that he could not allow the Supreme Court decision to be deliberately flouted. Therefore he sent 1,000 paratroopers and summoned 10,000 National Guardsmen to federal duty to enforce the ruling, and a token military force remained there for the rest of the year as protection for the black children. Note the picture on p. 749.

1964, Twenty-fourth Amendment. A consitutional change which outlawed state poll taxes in federal elections. A poll tax was a tax on persons as a requirement for voting. It was often used in southern states to keep poor blacks from voting.

1964, Civil Rights Act. This act outlawed discrimination in all places of public accommodation, such as restaurants, hotels, and theaters. It also prohibited discrimination in the application of voting laws and in the use of federal funds, which could be withheld from public schools refusing to desegregate. The act also established the Equal Employment Opportunities Commission (EEOC) to prevent discrimination in employment based on race or sex.

The Mexican-American

Bracero. A Mexican laborer who was permitted to enter the United States and work for a limited period of time. Special permits were issued to these individuals during World War II, when labor was in short supply, and again between 1948 and 1965, when additional farm workers were needed. *Bracero* is a Spanish term for manual laborer, one who works with his arms *(brazos)*.

Wetback. A Mexican laborer who illegally crosses the border. The term is derived from the fact that many wade or swim across the Rio Grande River between Mexico and Texas. If captured by the immigration authorities, the wetback is deported to Mexico.

Chicano. A term used by more militant Mexican-Americans to refer to themselves. The Chicanos demanded better educational opportunities, formed political organizations and parties, and encouraged Mexican-Americans to be proud of their traditions and culture.

OTHER TERMS TO IDENTIFY

1948 Election. There were four presidential candidates in this election, three of them Democrats. Governor Thomas Dewey of New York was the Republican candidate, and the incumbent, Truman, was nominated by the Democrats. Southern conservatives who disliked Truman's policies to help the nation's blacks formed the States' Rights or Dixiecrat party and nominated J. Strom Thurmond of South Carolina. The liberals, opposing Truman's foreign policy of containment and urging greater cooperation with the Soviet Union, formed the Progressive party and nominated former Vice-president Henry Wallace. Although public opinion polls indicated that Dewey would win, Truman won an amazing upset victory in November 1948.

Warren Commission. A seven-man commission appointed by President Johnson and headed by Chief Justice Earl Warren to investigate the assassination of President Kennedy. The commission established the sole responsibility of Lee Harvey Oswald for the killing and refuted rumors of plots by communist agents or right-wing organizations.

Barry M. Goldwater (1919–   ). A conservative Republican senator from Arizona who unsuccessfully ran for president against Johnson in 1964. As a leader of the right wing, he advocated a reduction of the authority of the national government in domestic matters and a commitment to total victory over world communism in foreign policy.

George Meany (1894–   ). A New York plumber who became president of the AFL in 1952 and has been president of the AFL-CIO since the two unions merged in 1955. Meany has frequently been courted by political leaders trying to gain the labor vote, and because of his position, he can exert a powerful influence on the economy.

Thurgood Marshall (1908–   ). Black lawyer who became head of the legal staff of the National Association for the Advancement of Colored People in 1938 and who successfully argued the *Brown* v. *Board of Education of Topeka* case before the Supreme Court in 1954. In 1967, Marshall became the first black to be appointed to the Supreme Court.

J. Robert Oppenheimer (1904–1967). Nuclear physicist who directed the development of the atom bomb at Los Alamos, New Mexico, during World War II. In 1953 he was suspended from the Atomic Energy Commission as a security risk on the ground that he had associated with certain communists and communist sympathizers. This case was an example of the hysteria of the McCarthy era.

Apportionment. The distribution of representatives in a legislative body based on population. In 1962 and 1964 the Supreme Court handed down decisions requiring district lines to be redrawn for the state legislatures and for the House of Representatives in order to insure the principle of "one man, one vote." As more people moved to cities and district lines remained the same, the urban areas had become underrepresented. Reapportionment was required to correct this inequity.

White Citizens Councils. Organizations formed, primarily in the South, to oppose the desegregation of public schools. These groups began to organize almost immediately after the Supreme Court decision *Brown* v. *Board of Education of Topeka* was handed down in 1954.

1961, Twenty-third Amendment. The constitutional amendment which gave the vote in presidential elections to residents of Washington, D.C.; that is, the federal district could have presidential electors. The District of Columbia is not a state, and therefore these individuals had not previously had the suffrage.

GLOSSARY

civil rights. Rights belonging to a person by virtue of his status as a citizen. The term refers to the constitutional rights of all United States citizens, including communists, women, and racial or ethnic minority groups. In recent years the phrase "civil rights movement" has often been used in a more limited sense to refer to efforts to win equality for the American black.

closed shop. An industry or business requiring new workers to join the union before they could be employed. The Taft-Hartley Act outlawed the closed shop. However, the law did permit union-shop contracts which forced new workers to join the union after accepting employment.

conservative. One who resists change and wants to maintain the existing order. In politics, conservatives generally prefer that the state governments accept more responsibility rather than the national government, and this tendency is referred to as supporting strong states' rights. In fact conservatives prefer as little government interference as possible in regulating the economy and in administering public welfare programs such as housing or medicine. In foreign policy, such individuals usually have pronounced anticommunism sentiments and favor a strong military.

Don Quixote. The hero of a tale written by the Spaniard Miguel de Cervantes Saavedra in the early 1600s, which was a satire on chivalry. Don Quixote was an idealistic, impractical romantic, often taking on impossible tasks. In one episode he attempted to do battle with a windmill. This incident is recalled in the political cartoon on p. 744, showing President Truman unsuccessfully fighting the passage of the Taft-Hartley Act.

draft. The selection of a person from a group for a particular duty. A presidential draft takes place when a person who has not really run for the position is nominated anyway to be his party's candidate. The selection of Adlai Stevenson to be the Democratic presidential candidate in 1952 was one of the few genuine drafts in the history of American political conventions.

egghead. Slang word for an intellectual. The term originally applied to an intellectual who supported bald-headed Adlai Stevenson in the 1952 election.

ever-normal granary concept. The idea that the country should not have to suffer because of years in which there was a bad harvest of certain farm products. Instead, surpluses should be stored by the government and distributed when needed, thus maintaining a stable supply.

filibuster. Making long speeches, often about irrelevant material, in order to delay legislative action. For example, a senator might stand up and read aloud the Washington, D.C., telephone directory rather than yield the floor to a senator who might call for a vote on a controversial issue. During the Truman Administration anti-poll tax and antilynching legislation designed to help the black was filibustered to death in the Senate.

GOP. The initials stand for Grand Old Party, referring to the Republican party. The phrase was first used in Republican campaign speeches in 1880.

jurisdictional conflicts between unions. Questions over which unions should be allowed to enroll members engaged in certain occupations. For example, in the late 1930s disputes arose between the AFL carpenters and the CIO woodworkers and also the AFL meatcutters and the CIO packinghouse workers.

Keynesian approach. The economic theories advocated by the British economist John Maynard Keynes (1883–1946), who felt that the government should deal with economic depression, not by trying to balance the budget, but by increasing the supply of money in circulation through cutting taxes, easing credit, and expanding public works programs.

lynch. To execute without due process of law, especially to hang someone. In the South the legal rights of blacks were not always observed, and Truman advocated a federal antilynching law to protect them. It did not pass.

Progressive party. The name of three separate splinter parties which have run presidential candidates. In 1912 Theodore Roosevelt broke with the Republicans and formed the Progressive or Bull Moose party. In 1924 Robert La Follette attracted liberals to a new Progressive party. And third, in 1948, Henry A. Wallace broke with the Democrats and formed a liberal Progressive party which favored closer cooperation with the Soviet Union.

reactionary. An ultraconservative who not only opposes change, but may want to revert to an earlier way of doing things.

red herring. Something which draws attention from the issue at hand.

Truman tried to dismiss the accusations against former communist Alger Hiss as a red herring designed by the Republicans to discredit his administration. The term is derived from the fact that the red herring was used to distract hunting dogs from the scent.

scarcity economics. The New Deal philosophy that creating a shortage of a product would cause the price to go up. Therefore crops were plowed under and cattle and hogs were slaughtered rather than sent to market. The Americans for Democratic Action rejected New Deal scarcity economics and felt expansion and economic growth were the key to prosperity.

secondary boycott. A boycott is the process of not using, buying, or dealing with a product as a form of protest. For example, one might not purchase grapes as a method of showing sympathy for the farm workers' union. However, if one also refused to shop at a store which carried these grapes, that would be considered a secondary boycott. Unions were forbidden to publicize secondary boycotts under the Taft-Hartley Act.

Waterloo. The town in Belgium where Napoleon was decisively defeated in 1815. Then he was sent as a prisoner of war to the island of Saint Helena, a British colony in the south Atlantic. Senator Robert Taft denounced the trials and execution of some Nazi leaders after World War II and felt they should have been simply imprisoned so as to avert more trouble, as had been done with Napoleon after Waterloo.

WORDS TO KNOW

Define the following, using the dictionary if necessary.

appellation	omnidirectional
cyclotron	prognosticators
endomorphic	scatological
inveterate	syntax
nefarious	unctuous

SAMPLE QUESTIONS

Multiple Choice

1. For the 1948 election, conservative Democrats opposed to Truman's civil rights measures formed the:
   a. States' Rights party.
   b. Progressive party.
   c. Americans for Democratic Action.
   d. Raza Unida party.
2. The AFL and the CIO:

   a. have always been separate.

   b. merged in 1955.

   c. were once joined but split over the 1964 election.

   d. still follow Gompers' leadership.

3. The Taft-Hartley Act:

   a. was sponsored by the Democracts.

   b. provided for a "cooling off" period in certain labor disputes.

   c. was favored by President Truman.

   d. all of the above.

4. Segregation was "inherently unequal" according to the Supreme Court decision of:

   a. *Yates* v. *U.S.*

   b. *Dred Scott* v. *Sanford.*

   c. *Plessy* v. *Ferguson.*

   d. *Brown* v. *Board of Education of Topeka.*

5. Racial discrimination in all places of public accommodation was outlawed by:

   a. *Brown* v. *Board of Education of Topeka.*

   b. the Twenty-third Amendment.

   c. Civil Rights Act of 1964.

   d. McCarran Internal Security Act.

True-False

1. The GI Bill of Rights granted veterans the right to form their own union.
2. Eisenhower's soil bank program fostered conservation and paid farmers not to plant.
3. *Braceros* formed a union within the AFL-CIO.
4. Reapportionment, the Twenty-third Amendment, and the Twenty-fourth Amendment were all designed to benefit the voter.
5. Robert Taft and Adlai Stevenson were members of the same political party.

ANSWERS
Multiple Choice: a, b, d, c. True-False: F, T, F, T, F.

30

Modern American Society

CHRONOLOGY

1957 Sputnik launched
1963 *The Feminine Mystique* by Betty Friedan
1964 Economic Opportunity Act
1965 Watts riots
1968 Martin Luther King assassinated

CHAPTER CHECKLIST

Changing society. American population shifted westward, and by 1963 California was more populous than New York state. Geographic mobility was stimulated by improvements in transportation, such as high-speed freeways for cars and the jetliner, first used in 1958. These facilities made the country seem smaller, and more social and cultural uniformity emerged, partly as an outgrowth of the growing middle class. A new popular enthusiasm for culture also appeared.

Literature

Paperbacks. Books bound in paper rather than with a hard cover. They were inexpensive, easy to carry, and were sold in all types of stores. After World War II, paperbacks became increasingly popular.

John Dos Passos (1896–1970). A Harvard-educated writer whose most famous work was a trilogy entitled *U.S.A.* (1930–1936). In it, Dos Passos portrayed American society between 1900 and 1930 in a cold, utterly realistic style and advanced an anticapitalist, pessimistic point of view. By the 1950s, however, he abandoned his leftist views and became a conservative, opposing the welfare state.

John Steinbeck (1902–1968). A novelist who realistically described the conditions in which the downtrodden lived and worked and who treated his characters with compassion. Steinbeck's most famous work, *The Grapes of Wrath* (1939), was about a poverty-stricken Oklahoma family who moved to California and became migrant fruit pickers.

Thomas Wolfe (1900–1938). A writer who grew up in Asheville, North Carolina, and whose novels, including *Look Homeward, Angel: A Story of the Buried Life* (1929), were largely autobiographical. Wolfe ably described contemporary society and the wide variety of American life.

William Faulkner (1897–1962). One of the finest modern American writers, who grew up in Mississippi and wrote about the South in such novels as *The Sound and the Fury* (1929) and *Sanctuary* (1931), which won a Pulitzer prize. Faulkner not only dealt with the poverty and pride of the American South, but also with universal dilemmas of modern life.

Painting

Abstract expressionism. A style of painting developed in the 1940s and 1950s in the United States. Artists who favored this form were subjective in their work; that is, they painted feelings and ideas from within themselves rather than representations of objects in the world. Outstanding abstract expressionists included Jackson Pollock and Mark Rothko.

Op art. A style of painting in which colors and geometric designs were used to produce dynamic optical effects.

Pop art. A style of art which often satirized American mass culture. Painters such as Andy Warhol created huge representations of everyday objects such as Campbell soup cans, and other painters did blowups of comic-strip characters. Both op and pop artists made use of modern technology such as spray guns and fluorescent paints.

Technology and Culture

Movies. The motion picture appeared around 1900. Some early silent classics were the eight-minute *The Great Train Robbery* (1903) and David Griffith's *Birth of a Nation* (1915). Talking movies were introduced with *The Jazz Singer* (1927), and million-dollar extravaganzas soon followed. Most movies of the period were designed for mindless entertainment.

Radio. Developed at the turn of the century and perfected by Lee De Forest before World War I, the radio industry quickly expanded after 1920 when the first commercial station began broadcasting in Pittsburgh. The radio provided entertainment at home, instant news coverage, and a wide audience for advertisers.

Television. A visual form of home entertainment which displayed the best and worst of radio's characteristics. News was promptly reported, and advertisers spent large sums of money to reach television's wide audience. But programming was often mediocre, and some felt that the news coverage held too much sway over public opinion.

Federal Communications Commission. An independent executive agency established in 1934. It has a seven-member board, appointed by the president and approved by the Senate, and the commissioners serve for seven years. They have jurisdiction over the cable, telephone, telegraph, radio, and television industries.

Poverty

Appalachia. The region extending approximately from Pittsburgh, Pennsylvania, to Birmingham, Alabama, which includes the largest area of rural poverty in the United States. The Appalachian Mountain area is chronically depressed, although it is rich in undeveloped natural resources.

1964, Economic Opportunity Act. The first major piece of legislation in President Johnson's war on poverty program. It included such provisions as the Job Corps, to provide educational and on-the-job training for youths between 16 and 21. The act established VISTA (Volunteers in Service to America), sometimes called the domestic Peace Corps, to staff antipoverty programs. Project Head Start, a preschool educational program for disadvantaged youngsters was also funded. The act included a wide variety of programs from small business loans to work-study grants.

The Black and Race Relations

Martin Luther King, Jr. (1929–1968). A Baptist preacher and nonviolent civil rights leader who won the Nobel Peace Prize in 1964. King was president of the Southern Christian Leadership Conference and led numerous peaceful demonstrations against segregation. He was a leader of the 1963 March on Washington, where he delivered his eloquent "I Have a Dream" speech. In 1968 he went to Memphis, Tennessee, to help striking garbage collectors, and was assassinated there on April 4.

Bus boycott. A refusal by blacks in Montgomery, Alabama, in 1955–1956, to continue to ride segregated buses. The boycott was incited by the arrest of a black woman, Mrs. Rosa Parks, who refused to give up her seat on the bus. This action was led by Martin Luther King, Jr., and culminated in a Supreme Court ruling which forced Montgomery to desegregate its public transportation system.

Lunch counter sit-ins. Attempts to desegregate lunch counters at five-and-tens or drugstores. This method was successfully used in 1961 when four black students in Greensboro, North Carolina, sat down at a segregated lunch counter and refused to leave when they were denied service. The Congress of Racial Equality (CORE) rushed field workers to Greensboro, and students in other southern towns copied the example of the sit-in. By late 1961 over a hundred lunch counters had been desegregated.

Freedom ride. A bus ride organized by the integrationists to test the effectiveness of federal regulations prohibiting discrimination in interstate transportation. The first freedom ride took place in 1961, when individuals, black and white, boarded buses in Washington, D.C., and traveled through the South, heading for New Orleans. They were harassed in several towns.

1963, March on Washington. A demonstration in which over 200,000 gathered in Washington, D.C., to voice their opposition to segregation and demand racial equality. Martin Luther King was one of its leaders.

Black Militancy

Black Muslims. Members of a black nationalist movement which favored racial separation and wanted a part of the United States set aside for the exclusive use of blacks. They practiced the religion of Islam and taught their members to distrust all whites. Elijah Muhammed became leader of the Black Muslims in 1934, and the movement had its headquarters in Chicago.

Malcolm X (1925–1965). A black who converted to the Black Muslim faith while in prison, and after his release, quickly moved up in the movement's hierarchy. However, conflict developed between Malcolm X and Elijah Muhammed, and in 1964 Malcolm X formed his own Organization of Afro-American Unity. This movement stressed the blacks' need to help themselves and to defend militantly their rights, but it also saw the crusade as part of a larger struggle to help oppressed people everywhere. In 1965 Malcolm X was assassinated by Black Muslim gunmen. See the picture of Malcolm X on p. 770.

1965, Watts riot. A violent demonstration of black frustration which lasted six days in Watts, a Los Angeles black ghetto. The riot was sparked by a policeman's halting a black motorist and trying to give him a sobriety test to determine if he was drunk. Protesting blacks poured into the street, and burning and looting followed. Fifteen thousand National Guardsmen were called in to assist the police, and order was finally restored after much bloodshed and property damage.

Kerner Commission. A committee appointed by President Johnson after the murder of Dr. Martin Luther King in 1968 to investigate racial conflicts and in particular the race riots of the 1960s. The group was headed by Governor Otto Kerner of Illinois and concluded that in general, rioters were expressing frustration at a system which denied them equal opportunities. They employed violence not so much as a method of forcing change, but simply to destroy the surroundings they could no longer tolerate.

Black Panthers. A militant black organization which was started in 1966 in Oakland, California, by Bobby Seale and Huey P. Newton. They were soon joined by Eldridge Cleaver, a convict on parole, whom they nominated for president in 1968. The Panthers demanded public compensation, that is, monetary payments from individuals and the government, for injustices done to blacks in the past. They set up armed headquarters around the nation and claimed they would defend themselves if attacked by police. In 1972 the Panthers supposedly discontinued their armed-defense tactics and moved into black community-development programs, with Seale unsuccessfully running for mayor of Oakland in 1973.

The Chicano

César Chávez (1927–   ). Mexican-American labor leader who heads the United Farm Workers Organizing Committee, which he founded in 1962. It is composed primarily of migrant workers and is affiliated with the AFL-CIO. Chávez gained nationwide recognition between 1965–1970, when he helped the California grape pickers eventually win recognition of their union after a series of sit-ins, marches, and a national, consumer boycott of grapes. Note the picture of Chávez on p. 773.

Women's Liberation

Betty Friedan (1921–   ). A leader of the women's liberation movement who formed the National Organization of Women (NOW) in 1966 and served as its first president (1966–1970). She first became nationally prominent with the publication of a best-selling book, *The Feminine Mystique* (1963), which stated that there was a mystique that women found fulfillment only in the roles of wife, mother, and homemaker and that this mystique was being perpetuated by business, the press, and educators. According to Friedan, these ideas contributed to much frustration on the part of women who could not adapt to that supposed ideal, and woman's image must be changed.

Civil Rights Act of 1964. Outlawed job discrimination based on sex as well as on race. As a result, government agencies and the courts put pressure on employers to provide equal opportunities for women.

Equal Rights Amendment. A proposed amendment to the Constitution which states that there can be no discrimination based on sex. It passed both houses of Congress in 1972, and must be ratified within seven years by three-fourths of the states before it can go into effect.

Education

"Educationists." Educators who felt that the purpose of schools was to promote the emotional development of the student. They de-emphasized academic subjects and concentrated on the "adjustment" of the child. This point of view came into vogue after World War I.

"Traditionalists." Educators who emphasized excellence in academic subject matter. Their viewpoint became more popular after Russia lauched the first earth satellite, *Sputnik,* in 1957, and some thought we were falling behind in the space race because of inadequate educational preparation, particularly in science and math.

1958, National Defense Education Act. The government allocated funds to upgrade work in the sciences and foreign languages, to expand guidance services, and to experiment with televison and other teaching devices.

1964, Berkeley Student Strike. A demonstration of unrest and dissatisfaction on the University of California campus at Berkeley. The students held sit-ins, that is, occupied buildings and prevented normal activities from continuing over a period of weeks. Clark Kerr, president of the University of California system, resigned. This incident was similar to signs of unrest among the student population on other campuses during the 1960s.

Students for a Democratic Society (SDS). An organization of liberal, idealistic students who were disillusioned with the American establishment. Its members led student demonstrations, mostly sit-ins, against racism, poverty, and United States involvement in the Vietnam conflict. This movement reached its peak in 1968 and then began to decline in influence.

Sexual Revolution

Changing attitudes. Conventional ideas about premarital sex, and about contraception and abortion, about homosexuality, and about pornography were openly challenged in the late 1960s. More sexual freedom contributed to the sharp increase in the divorce rate and also to the revival in the women's rights movement.

Alfred C. Kinsey (1894–1956). Professor of zoology at the University of Indiana who published *Sexual Behavior in the Human Male* (1948) and *Sexual Behavior in the Human Female* (1953). These books were based on thousands of interviews conducted by Kinsey and his associates and revealed that a greater variety of sexual activities commonly took place than was generally talked about.

OTHER TERMS TO IDENTIFY

National Aeronautics and Space Agency (NASA). An agency created by the government in 1958 to conduct research and to coordinate space probes and manned flights in space. NASA was well funded in the 1960s but then began to experience cutbacks in expenditures and in public enthusiasm.

Charlie Chaplin (1889–1977). A British actor and director who became a hit comic in American movies beginning in 1914. His most famous character portrayal was the "little tramp" as shown in the painting on p. P6 •15. In 1952 Chaplin moved to Switzerland because of tax difficulties with the United States government.

Black Power. A slogan adopted in 1966 by black militants expressing their intention to do without help from whites in the fight for black rights. The term was popularized by Stokely Carmichael, chairman of the Student Nonviolent Coordinating Committee (SNCC).

Crusade for Justice. A militant Mexican-American group interested in achieving social reforms and organizing political action groups. Its slogan was *Venceremos,* Spanish for "We shall overcome," and its leader was Rodolfo "Corky" Gonzales.

James Conant (1893–1978). An educator who taught chemistry (1916–1933) at Harvard and then became its president (1933–1953). His later work centered on education, especially at the high-school level. In *The Child, the Parent, and the State* (1959) he recommended increased emphasis on mathematics and foreign languages. *Slums and Suburbs* (1961) warned against the effects of two school systems, one for the poor and one for the privileged. In *The Education of American Teachers* (1963) he stressed the need for more academic subject courses in teacher training programs. Because of his views, Conant was considered a "traditionalist rather than an "educationist."

GLOSSARY

black separatism. The creed of some militant blacks that blacks must not become integrated or assimilated into the white culture but must maintain their own traditions. Carrying this idea to an extreme, the Black Muslim movement demanded that a part of the United States be set aside for the exclusive use of the blacks.

blue-collar worker. A wage earner with a job performed in rough clothing and often involving manual labor, such as a factory or construction laborer. During the 1960s many blue-collar workers moved up socially and economically and were considered part of the middle class.

consensus. Collection opinion or general agreement. Many Americans in the 1960s seemed intent on simply following or reflecting the general climate of opinion rather than thinking for themselves.

de facto. In reality or fact, but not necessarily legal. In the 1960s school boycotts were held to protest the de facto segregation that existed in predominantly black neighborhoods.

demographer. One who studies the characteristics of human population, such as size, growth, density, and distribution. Demographers in the 1970s watched with interest the declining birth rate and its possible effects on society.

Mohandas Gandhi (1869–1948). A political leader of India who became known for his campaigns of civil disobedience expressed in nonviolent resistance to the laws. The technique of nonviolent civil disobedience was adopted by some civil rights leaders, including Martin Luther King, Jr.

ham. A government-licensed amateur radio operator who talks to other ham operators as a hobby.

horse opera. A term used jokingly to refer to a film or other theatrical work about the American West.

male chauvinism. Male behavior, according to women liberationists, that has led to women's oppression.

manual dexterity. Skill in the use of the hands. Modern industries employed increasing numbers of women because much of the work demanded manual dexterity rather than strength.

median. The middle value in a distribution, above and below which is an equal number of values. The median income for the nation was $10,000 a year.

melting pot. A place where immigrants of different cultures or races form an integrated society. Ethnic diversity continues to exist, however, in the so-called American "melting pot."

Murphy bed. A bed that folds or swings into a closet for concealment. It was named after its American inventor, William Laurence Murphy (1876–1959). A picture of Charlie Chaplin trying to climb on a folding Murphy bed is on p. 765.

numbers racket. A lottery, illegally conducted, in which bets may be wagered on the appearance of unpredictable numbers, such as on the last digits in the pari-mutuel racing totals for the day. Malcolm Little, later known as Malcolm X, lived for several years on the edge of the underworld in New York's Harlem, working in the numbers racket.

Pulitzer prize. Annual awards for achievements in American journalism, literature, and music. The prizes are paid for from the income of a trust left by the newspaper publisher, Joseph Pulitzer, and have been awarded since 1917.

Samson. An Israelite judge of extraordinary strength who was betrayed to his enemies, the Philistines, by Delilah. Samson was strong because of his vows to God, symbolized in his long hair, and when Delilah cut his hair his strength was gone. Captured and blinded, and chained in the temple of the Philistines, he regained his strength as his hair grew long again, and with his bare hands he pulled down the temple, destroying himself along with his enemies. In the ghetto riots, blacks behaved like Samson, destroying their hated surroundings even though it meant self-destruction.

Sputnik. Any of the artificial earth satellites launched by the Soviet Union, especially the first which went into orbit on October 4, 1957. The Russian word means "fellow traveler (of Earth)." The launching of *Sputnik* caused many Americans to feel that the United States was suffering from a technological and education lag behind the Russians.

trilogy. A group of three dramatic or literary works related in subject or theme. Both John Dos Passos and James T. Farrell wrote trilogies in the 1930s.

welfare state. A country which supports the economic security of the majority of its citizens through such programs as the subsidization of housing and medical care, assistance to needy families, minimum wage legislation, pensions for the aged, and insurance against unemployment.

WORDS TO KNOW

Define the following, using the dictionary if necessary.

abstemious   parietal
apocalyptic   septuagenarian
kaleidoscopic   spacial
mélange   syncretistic
nihilistic   vignettes

SAMPLE QUESTIONS

Multiple Choice

1. Bus boycotts, lunch counter sit-ins, and freedom rides were all attempts to promote:
   a. integration.
   b. black separatism.
   c. academic freedom.
   d. segregation.
2. Which of the following is *not* correctly matched?
   a. students: Berkeley strike.
   b. migrant workers: grape pickers strike.
   c. Indians: occupation of Wounded Knee.
   d. Chicanos: Watts riot.
3. Which of the following is *not* correctly matched?
   a. Malcolm X: Organization of Afro-American Unity.
   b. Elijah Muhammed: Student Nonviolent Coordinating Committee.
   c. Bobby Seale: Black Panthers.
   d. Martin Luther King: Southern Christian Leadership Conference.
4. Which of the following is *not* correctly matched?
   a. Jackson Pollock: art.
   b. Charlie Chaplin: movies.
   c. William Faulkner: literature.
   d. James Conant: radio.
5. Which of the following is *not* correctly matched?
   a. Alfred Kinsey: *Sexual Behavior in the Human Male.*
   b. Betty Friedan: *The Feminine Mystique.*
   c. John Steinbeck: *The Grapes of Wrath.*
   d. Thomas Wolfe: *The American High School Today.*

True-False

1. The Kerner Commission determined that the purpose behind race riots was to kill particular white politicians.

2. Johnson's war on poverty was initiated with the National Defense Education Act.
3. The Federal Communications Commission has the authority to regulate the telephone, radio, and television industries.
4. Martin Luther King and Eldridge Cleaver used very different techniques in their attempts to better the position of the black.
5. The Civil Rights Act outlawed discrimination based on sex.

Multiple Choice: a, d, b, d. True-False: F, F, T, T, T.
ANSWERS

31

Vietnam and Its Aftermath

CHRONOLOGY

1964 Gulf of Tonkin Resolution
1972 Watergate break-in
1973 Withdrawal from Vietnam
1973 Vice-President Agnew resigned
1973 Oil embargo
1974 President Nixon resigned

CHAPTER CHECKLIST

War in Vietnam

1954–1964, Limited involvement. After the French withdrew in 1954, the United States sent military advisers to bolster South Vietnam's anticommunist regime. But rebel forces, called Vietcong, which received supplies from communist North Vietnam and indirectly from China and the Soviet Union, increased in strength and controlled large sections of the country.

1964, Gulf of Tonkin Resolution. After some North Vietnamese gunboats fired on American destroyers in the Gulf of Tonkin (see map on p. 785), President Johnson encouraged Congress to pass a resolution which authorized him to "repel any armed attack against the forces to the United States and to prevent further aggression." Early in 1965 Johnson sent in combat troops and permitted air attacks on both South and North Vietnam. War was never officially declared by Congress, but Johnson based his actions on the Gulf of Tonkin Resolution.

Doves vs. hawks. Critics of United States involvement in Vietnam were called doves, whereas supporters of the war were called hawks.

The Election of 1968

Republican: Richard Nixon
Democratic: Hubert Humphrey
American Independent: George Wallace

Eugene McCarthy (1916–   ). Senator from Wisconsin who made opposition to the Vietnam conflict his campaign issue for the Democratic primaries. His success in New Hampshire and Wisconsin was a factor in causing President Johnson to withdraw from the race.

Robert Kennedy (1925–1968). Former attorney general and Democratic senator from New York, Kennedy reversed his earlier position and decided to enter the race, also as an opponent to Johnson's war policy. After narrowly defeating McCarthy in the California primary, Kennedy was assassinated in a Los Angeles hotel by Sirhan Sirhan, a young Arab nationalist who had been angered by Kennedy's support of Israel.

Democratic Convention in Chicago. Hundreds of radical demonstrators gathered in front of the convention building to put pressure on the delegates to repudiate Johnson's Vietnam policy. Violent clashes broke out between the protestors and Chicago police, and millions watched on television newscasts. With the backing of President Johnson, Vice-President Hubert Humphrey won the nomination, and support of the Vietnam war policy was included as a plank in the party platform.

George Wallace (1919–   ). Democratic governor of Alabama who formed his own American Independent party which attracted wide southern and conservative support. He stood for "law and order" and opposed forced desegregation of schools. Wallace hoped to win enough electoral votes to prevent either major party from obtaining a majority, thus throwing the election into the House. There the representatives would choose from the top three candidates, and the Democratic and Republican candidates would probably bargain with Wallace to get him to swing his supporters to one of them. Wallace's strategy did not work in 1968, but he started campaigning again in 1972 and was shot by an assailant, leaving him partially paralyzed.

RICHARD MILHOUSE NIXON (1913–   ), 37th President

Born in California and graduated from Whittier College and Duke Law School.
Republican representative from California (1947–1951).
Senator (1951–1953).
Vice-president under Eisenhower (1953–1961).
Unsuccessful candidate for president (1960) and for governor of California (1962).
President (1969–1974).
Resigned on August 9, 1974, under threat of impeachment.

Nixon as President

Wage and price controls. In order to combat spiraling inflation, Nixon used a 1970 law giving the president power to control prices and wages. The new economic plan, which went into effect in the summer of 1971, had three phases:

Phase I. A 90-day price and wage freeze. In addition, a 10 percent surcharge was placed on imports in an attempt to get Americans to buy United States products, so as to ease the deficit in the balance of trade.

Phase II. Wage and price increases were limited by a newly created Pay Board and a Price Commission. This phase lasted from late 1971 to early 1973.

Phase III. Wage and price controls ended, and voluntary "restraints" (except in the areas of food, health care, and construction) were called for. However, the plea for "self-control" did not work, and prices soared.

Nominations to Supreme Court. The Constitution states that the president may appoint justices of the Supreme Court but that they must be confirmed by a vote in the Senate. In 1969 Nixon had an opportunity to nominate a justice when Abe Fortas resigned under fire. His first two nominees, Judge Clement Haynesworth, Jr., of South Carolina, and Judge G. Harrold Carswell of Florida were rejected by the Senate, and Nixon felt the rejections were maneuvered by "liberal" senators who disliked southern conservatives. His third choice, Harry Blackmun of Minnesota, won the unanimous approval of the Senate. The rejection of the first two nominees, however, definitely damaged Nixon's prestige.

Diplomatic visits abroad. Summit meetings with the heads of the two major communist powers, China and the USSR, were arranged by Nixon's principal foreign policy adviser, Henry Kissinger. The visits indicated that the countries were willing to improve relations.

February 1972: China. Nixon flew to Peking to consult with Premier Chou En-lai and other Chinese leaders. See the picture on p. 793. The meeting was significant because it marked the renewal of diplomatic contact between the two countries which had ceased when Mao Tsetung's communist government was established in 1949. Full diplomatic recognition did not follow, that is, ambassadors were not exchanged, but lower-ranking diplomatic officials were accepted and other contacts developed.

May 1972: Union of Soviet Socialist Republics. Nixon made a goodwill trip to Moscow. One result was the signing of a treaty limiting strategic missiles.

Vietnam

Paris peace negotiations. Talks began in May 1968, between the United States and North Vietnam. When Nixon became president in 1969, the talks were expanded to include representatives of South Vietnam and the Vietcong. The North Vietnamese insisted on the unconditional withdrawal of all United States forces.

Vietnamization. The United States strategy of trying to build up the South Vietnamese army so that American troops could withdraw without allowing the communists to overrun South Vietnam. Americans had been implementing this strategy since the French had pulled out in 1954, but with little success. However, in 1969 Nixon stepped up efforts at Vietnamization and by the end of the year had withdrawn 60,000 American soldiers.

1969, Vietnam Moratorium Day. A nationwide antiwar demonstration organized primarily by students which took place on October 15. The following month a second Moratorium Day was held, and 250,000 people marched past the White House to protest United States involvement in Vietnam. These demonstrations reflected the growing antiwar sentiment.

1970, Invasion of Cambodia. Nixon announced that military intelligence had indicated enemy forces were using neutral Cambodia to consolidate their troops and supplies. Therefore he ordered thousands of troops into Cambodia to destroy these bases and resumed the bombing of targets in North Vietnam. This escalation of the war effort heightened antiwar feeling, especially among students, and hundreds of campuses closed down as a result of student protests.

Final negotiations. In the summer of 1972 Henry Kissinger began serious negotiations in Paris, and by October a proposed settlement had been hammered out. Shortly before the November presidential election, Kissinger announced that peace was "at hand." However, in December Nixon stated that the North Vietnamese were not bargaining in good faith, and he ordered the resumption of bombing in North Vietnam.

January 1973: Paris Peace Agreement. The North Vietnamese retained control of sections of South Vietnam. They agreed to release American prisoners of war within 60 days, and when this was accomplished, the last American troops were withdrawn from Vietnam.

1972 Election

Republican: Richard Nixon

Democrat: George McGovern

Nixon won a landslide victory, carrying all but Massachusetts and Washington, D.C. McGovern's campaign was hurt by conflict over the vice-presidency. His first running mate, Senator Thomas Eagleton, was forced to resign when it was learned that he had once undergone shock treatments for psychological depression. McGovern's next choice was Sargeant Shriver, former Peace Corps head and Ambassador to France, and also a brother-in-law of John and Robert Kennedy.

Watergate

June 17, 1972: Watergate break-in. James McCord, a former FBI agent, and four other men broke into the Democratic headquarters at the Watergate, an apartment and office complex in Washington, D.C. The burglars were caught going through party files and installing electronic eavesdropping devices. All the defendants except McCord pleaded guilty, and he was convicted by a jury. Before Judge John Sirica imposed sentences, John McCord wrote him a letter claiming that high Republican officials had known in advance about the break-in and had persuaded most of the defendants to keep their connection secret. It was later learned that large sums of money had been paid to the families of the defendants in order to insure the burglars' silence.

Ervin Committee. A special Senate investigating committee, headed by Senator Sam Ervin, Jr., of North Carolina, heard testimony about the Watergate affair and about possible attempts by high government officials to cover up the details. Many of these sessions were televised in the summer of 1973. Jeb Stuart Magruder, head of the Committee to Re-elect the President (CREEP), admitted his involvement, as did White House lawyer James Dean, III, who claimed that President Nixon had participated in the cover up attempt, a charge that Nixon denied. During the Ervin hearings, the information also came out that the president systematically made secret tape recordings of conversations and telephone calls in his Oval Office in the White House. It was obvious that these tapes could establish the truth about White House involvement, but Nixon refused to release them, claiming "executive privilege."

Archibald Cox (1912–   ), special prosecutor. President Nixon appointed Professor Cox of the Harvard Law School to investigate the Watergate cover-up and promised his full cooperation. But Nixon balked when Cox demanded certain White House documents, including the tapes. Cox obtained a subpoena from Judge Sirica ordering Nixon to turn over the tapes. Nixon appealed, and the appellate court upheld Judge Sirica's order. The next step was for Nixon to appeal to the Supreme Court, but before the case reached the Court, Nixon decided to fire Cox.

> October 20, 1973: "Saturday night massacre." On this date Nixon ordered Attorney General Elliott Richardson to fire the special prosecutor, but Richardson resigned rather than do so. Assistant Attorney General William Ruckelshaus did likewise. But the solicitor general, third-ranking officer of the Justice Department, carried out Nixon's order. These events became popularly known as the "Saturday night massacre" and caused a loud outcry of public opinion.

Leon Jaworski (1905–   ), special prosecutor. Jaworski, a Houston attorney, was appointed by Nixon and confirmed by the Senate to replace Cox, and Nixon promised him access to whatever documents or tapes he needed. It was soon discovered, however, that some of the tapes were missing and that a section of another had been erased.

The Vice-Presidency

Spiro T. Agnew (1918–   ). Vice-president under Nixon (1969–1973) who resigned his position on October 10, 1973. Agnew was accused of having accepted bribes while county executive of Baltimore and governor of Maryland, and also of income tax evasion. After his resignation, Agnew was fined $10,000 for tax evasion and placed on three years probation.

Gerald R. Ford (1913–   ). Following the provisons of the Twenty-fifth Amendment, Nixon nominated Ford, the Republican minority leader in the House of Representatives, as vice-president, and he was confirmed by a majority vote in both houses of Congress.

Oil Embargo

The boycott. In late 1973, the Arab states cut off oil shipments to the United States, Japan, and most of western Europe in an attempt to get these countries to pressure Israel into withdrawing from land occupied in the 1967 "six-day" war. This embargo caused a serious energy crisis, and fuel prices soared. Finally, in the spring of 1974, Secretary of State Henry Kissinger negotiated a tentative agreement, first with Egypt and Israel, then with Syria and Israel, for the withdrawal of Israel from some of the occupied territory. Convinced of American goodwill, the Arab nations lifted the obycott. But oil prices remained high, further contributing to soaring inflation.

President Nixon's Problems

Income taxes. Nixon's opponents charged that he had paid almost no income taxes during his presidency. He published his 1969–1972 income tax returns showing that he had only paid about $1,600 in two years during which his income exceeded $500,000. The explanation was that he had taken huge deductions for the gift of some of his vice-presidential papers to the National Archives in Washington, D.C. After an audit by both the Internal Revenue Service (IRS) and a joint congressional committee, it was determined that most of the deductions were unjustified. The IRS assessed Nixon nearly half a million dollars in back taxes and interest.

White House tapes. In November 1973, Nixon turned over tapes to Judge Sirica with the understanding that relevant material would be presented to the grand jury investigating the Watergate affair. The following March, the grand jury indicted former White House staff chiefs John Ehrlichman and H. R. Haldeman, former Attorney General John Mitchell, who had been head of CREEP at the time of the break-in, and four other White House aides for conspiring to block the Watergate investigation. The jurors also named Nixon as an "unindicted co-conspirator." In an attempt to check public criticism, in April 1974, Nixon released edited transcripts of the tapes he had turned over to the grand jury. But instead, many individuals viewed the tapes as incriminating evidence, and some of Nixon's supporters demanded that he resign. To make matters worse, when the House judiciary committee received the actual tapes and checked them against the transcripts, it found that some material damaging to the president had been omitted from the transcripts. Additional tapes were demanded. Special Prosecutor Jaworski subpoenaed 64 tapes, and the Supreme Court ruled unanimously that the president must turn them over. The House judiciary committee, studying possible impeachment charges, unsuccessfully subpoenaed over 100.

Judiciary committee hearings. In the summer of 1974, the House judiciary committee, which was charged with making a recommendation to the full membership of the House, adopted three articles of impeachment. The articles accused the president of obstructing justice, misusing the powers of his office, and failing to obey the committee's subpoenas.

Resignation. When the Supreme Court, in *U.S.* v. *Richard M. Nixon,* ruled that the president must turn over the 64 requested tapes to Jaworski, the process of transcribing them began, and for the first time Nixon's lawyer, James St. Clair, heard the actual tapes. The tapes revealed that Nixon had participated in the Watergate cover-up, and when they were released on August 5, 1974, impeachment by the House and conviction by the Senate seemed almost a certainty. Consequently on August 8, Nixon wrote a letter of resignation to the secretary of state which became effective at noon on August 9.

GERALD RUDOLPH FORD (1913–   ), 38th President

Born in Nebraska and graduated from the University of Michigan and from Yale Law School.

Republican member of the House of Representatives from Michigan (1949–1973), and minority leader from 1964.

Vice-president under Nixon (1973–1974) after the resignation of Spiro T. Agnew.

Inaugurated as president on August 9, 1974, after the resignation of Richard Nixon.

President (1974–1977).

President Ford's Problems

Blanket presidential pardon to Nixon for crimes known and unknown criticized.

Economy slumped, and inflation increased.

South Vietnam fell to communist forces of North Vietnam, and thousands of refugees sought asylum in the United States.

American merchant ship *Mayaguez* captured by Cambodian naval forces. Ford demanded its release; Marines were sent in; and 38 died in the operation.

JAMES EARL CARTER, JR. (1924–   ), 39th President

Born in Plains, Georgia and graduated from the U.S. Naval Academy at Annapolis.
Democratic governor of Georgia (1970–1972).
President (1977–   ).

A Search for Meaning

George Bancroft (1800–1891). An historian who saw American history as the working out of God's plan, which he thought called for "the diffusion of intelligence among the masses" and the triumph of democracy.

Frederick Jackson Turner (1861–1932). An historian who explained American history in terms of the frontier which he felt had been a democratizing influence. Turner also stressed the importance of internal conflicts.

Charles A. Beard (1874–1948). An historian who saw the history of democracy in America as the sum of clashes between rival social and economic interests. One example was the clash at the 1787 Constitutional Convention between owners of land and owners of government securities.

David M. Potter (1910–1976). An historian who felt that the unique quality of American life was the result of material abundance made possible by the rich resources of the continent. This abundance had created a democratic and optimistic society.

Other modern historians. Some felt that the democratic system worked because of the degree of "consensus," the sameness of most Americans' objectives. "New Left" historians, on the other hand, pointed to the mistreatment of minorities and the extremes of wealth and poverty and insisted that the American government had never been truly democratic.

Two questions to ask about the future of the United States.
1. Has modern technology outstripped human intelligence?
2. Has our social development outstripped our emotional development?

OTHER TERMS TO IDENTIFY

February 1968: Tet offensive. A massive offensive launched by North Vietnam and the Vietcong against South Vietnamese cities. It was designed to coincide with the Lunar New Year (Tet). The communists successfully occupied part of the capital, Saigon, and completely captured other cities. They were eventually thrown back, but the temporary success discredited the American military, under William Westmoreland, which had claimed that the communists were almost defeated. The Tet offensive also affected the 1968 election primaries by swinging support to the antiwar candiate, Eugene McCarthy.

Daniel Ellsberg (1931–   ). Charged with espionage, theft, and conspiracy for making copies of a secret, 47-volume government study of the Vietnam war and releasing it to newspapers in 1971. Ellsberg had made copies of the report, known as the Pentagon papers, while working for the Rand Corporation in California in 1969. After the trial in 1973, the judge dismissed Ellsberg's case because of improper government conduct, including an illegal break-in by two agents at the office of Ellsberg's psychiatrist in an attempt to uncover possible derogatory information.

Henry Kissinger (1923–   ). A German-born American who became a professor at Harvard, President Nixon's chief foreign policy adviser during his first term, and secretary of state in 1973. Kissinger won the 1973 Nobel Peace Prize for negotiating the Vietnam cease-fire agreement.

Judge John J. Sirica (1904–   ). A federal judge since 1957 and chief judge of the U.S. District Court for the District of Columbia since 1971. Judge Sirica presided over the Watergate break-in investigation and the legal battles between the White House and the special prosecutors who subpoenaed presidential tapes.

GLOSSARY

cover-up. An attempt to hide or conceal an incident from the public. The Watergate cover-up refers to the attempt by high government officials to conceal their association with or knowledge of the break-in at the Democratic headquarters.

"credibility gap." A phrase applied in 1966 to public skepticism of the official reports released by President Johnson and members of his administration, particularly concerning the supposed progress and "victories" of the Vietnam war.

détente. A relaxation of military and diplomatic international tensions. It is a French word which means a "loosening." In the early 1970s, a détente in the relations between the United States and the Soviet Union developed.

devaluation. Reduction in the gold or silver content of the basic monetary unit. Since the United States no longer converts dollars to gold, when President Nixon devalued the dollar in 1971, he simply fixed the legal value of the currency at a lower level. One of the chief reasons for doing so was to reduce the value of the dollar in relation to the currency of other countries. This action meant that American products would sell more cheaply abroad and foreign products sold in the United States would be more expensive. The result would hopefully be a return to a favorable balance of trade, that is, exporting more than importing.

domino theory. A theory believed by President Eisenhower which stated that if the communists were allowed to take over one country, then its neighbors would fall, and so on, until the whole world was communist. Countries were like a row of dominoes: If one were pushed, the rest would topple. Eisenhower compared the situation to what had happened before World War II, when Hitler had been allowed to occupy one country after another in eastern Europe.

"easy money" policies. Programs which put a great deal of money into circulation. The term was used to refer to President Johnson's "war on poverty" programs and others which pumped money into the economy. President Nixon's policies were just the opposite, as he cut federal spending and tried to balance the budget.

executive privilege. A term used to refer to the special rights of the president and the executive branch as a result of constitutional provisions for separation of powers. For example, President Nixon refused to testify in court (judicial branch) and before congressional committees (legislative branch), claiming executive privilege. He also tried to extend executive privilege to include top members of the White House staff, such as H. R. Haldeman and John Erlichman, so that they would not have to testify before congressional investigating committees.

expletive deleted. Literally means that a curse word was left out. When edited transcripts of the White House tapes were released in 1974, the phrase "expletive deleted" was frequently seen, revealing to the public that Nixon often used profanity in his conversations.

grand jury. A jury of 12 to 23 convened to evaluate accusations against persons charged with having committed crime and to determine whether the evidence warrants indictment.

impeachment. To charge a government official formally with improper conduct while in office. In order to impeach the president, the House judiciary committee studies the charges and makes a recommendation to the full membership of the House of Representatives. A majority vote in the House is required to impeach; the case is tried before the Senate, with the chief justice presiding. If two-thirds of the senators vote to convict the president, he is removed from office.

impoundment. To hold something and refuse to release it. President Nixon impounded, that is, refused to spend, funds already appropriated by Congress. He hoped that cutting back on federal expenditures would slow inflation.

"New Left" historians. Historians concerned with the social and economic inequities in society. They point out the mistreatment of minority groups and the extremes of wealth and poverty, often indicating Marxist influence in their writings.

silent majority. A term first used by President Nixon in November 1969 to refer to the American people who supported him and his Vietnam war policies but who did not openly demonstrate.

strict constructionist. An individual who believes in a literal interpretation of the Constitution, de-emphasizing implied or inferred powers. A strict constructionist generally wishes to limit the powers of the national government. President Nixon appointed conservative "strict constructionists" to the Supreme Court.

subpoena. A written, legal order requiring a person to appear in court to give testimony or to turn over evidence.

Vietcong. A Vietnamese belonging to or supporting the communist National Liberation Front in South Vietnam. It is short for the Vietnamese phrase Viet Nam Cong Sam, which means Vietnamese communist.

WORDS TO KNOW

Define the following, using the dictionary if necessary.

adamantine	homilies
ancillary	napalm
defoliants	profligate
effete	sententiously
gauntlet	viziers

SAMPLE QUESTIONS

Multiple Choice

1. President Johnson was authorized to use armed force in Vietnam by:
   a. the Gulf of Tonkin Resolution.
   b. a congressional declaration of war.
   c. the Vietnamization policy.
   d. the Pentagon.
2. Who of the following was *not* hopeful for the Democratic nomination for the presidency in 1968?
   a. Hubert Humphrey.
   b. Eugene McCarthy.
   c. Robert Kennedy.
   d. George Wallace
3. Who of the following was *not* implicated in the Watergate scandals?
   a. John Dean, III.
   b. James McCord.
   c. Jeb Stuart Magruder.
   d. Elliot Richardson.

4. Which of the following was *not* a problem facing the nation in the mid 1970s?
   a. political scandals.
   b. inflation.
   c. fuel shortage.
   d. draft riots.
5. Who of the following did *not* have the assigned duty to learn the details of the Watergate cover-up?
   a. Sam Ervin.
   b. Archibald Cox.
   c. Henry Kissinger.
   d. Leon Jaworski.

True-False

1. Nixon was impeached by the House of Representatives and therefore had to resign.
2. Doves were critics of United States involvement in Vietnam.
3. Wage and price controls were designed to curb deflation.
4. The purpose of Moratorium Day was to protest Nixon's visits to China and Russia.
5. Gerald Ford became vice-president and then president because of the provisions in the Twenty-fifth Amendment.

ANSWERS
Multiple Choice: a, d, d, c. True-False: F, T, F, F, T.